MW00453884

COLLECTED WORKS OF RENÉ GUÉNON

INITIATION AND SPIRITUAL REALIZATION

RENÉ GUÉNON

INITIATION
AND SPIRITUAL
REALIZATION

Translator
Henry D. Fohr

Editor
Samuel D. Fohr

SOPHIA PERENNIS

HILLSDALE NY

Library of Congress Cataloging-in-Publication Data

Guénon, René
[Initiation et réalisation spirituelle. English]
Initiation and spiritual realization / René Guénon ; translated by
Henry D. Fohr ; edited by Samuel D. Fohr

p. cm. — (Collected works of René Guénon)
Includes index.
ISBN 0 900588 35 7 (pbk: alk. paper)
ISBN 0 900588 42 x (cloth: alk. paper)
1. Initiation rites—Religious aspects I. Fohr, S.D., 1943– II. Title
BL615.G5 2001
291.3'8—dc21   2001000438

THE PUBLISHER
GIVES SPECIAL THANKS TO
HENRY D. AND JENNIE L. FOHR
FOR MAKING THIS EDITION POSSIBLE

CONTENTS

EDITORIAL NOTE

THE PAST CENTURY HAS WITNESSED an erosion of earlier cultural values as well as a blurring of the distinctive characteristics of the world's traditional civilizations, giving rise to philosophic and moral relativism, multiculturalism, and dangerous fundamentalist reactions. As early as the 1920s, the French metaphysician René Guénon (1886–1951) had diagnosed these tendencies and presented what he believed to be the only possible reconciliation of the legitimate, although apparently conflicting, demands of outward religious forms, 'exoterisms', with their essential core, 'esoterism'. His works are characterized by a foundational critique of the modern world coupled with a call for intellectual reform; a renewed examination of metaphysics, the traditional sciences, and symbolism, with special reference to the ultimate unanimity of all spiritual traditions; and finally, a call to the work of spiritual realization. Despite their wide influence, translation of Guénon's works into English has so far been piecemeal. The *Sophia Perennis* edition is intended to fill the urgent need to present them in a more authoritative and systematic form. A complete list of Guénon's works, given in the order of their original publication in French, follows this note.

The present volume is a companion volume to *Perspectives on Initiation*, and in accordance with Guénon's wish was the first thematic collection of his writings published after his death. In *Perspectives*, Guénon defined the precise nature of initiation, which is essentially the transmission by appropriate rites of a spiritual influence intended to permit a being in the human state to attain the spiritual degree designated in several Traditions as the 'edenic state', thence to rise to higher states, and finally to what has been called both 'Deliverance' and the state of 'Supreme Identity'. *Initiation and Spiritual Realization* further clarifies these themes in several ways. The text falls naturally into four parts. The first examines the mental and psychological obstacles that may hinder comprehension of the initiatic point of view and the quest for initiation. The second clarifies and develops several key points concerning the nature of initiation and certain of its preconditions—one of the most commonly misunderstood being the need to conform to the essentials of a traditional exoterism. The third and in many respects most important part considers certain degrees of that spiritual realization which everything preceding it aims to make more easily understandable, and, to a certain degree, more easily accessible. And finally, the last three chapters, the real keys to both books, provide a comprehensive metaphysical account of the possibility of a total spiritual realization starting from our corporeal state, a realization that belonged by nature and function to the Divine Messengers called by the various traditions Prophet, Rasul, Bodhisattva, and Avatara..

Guénon often uses words or expressions set off in 'scare quotes'. To avoid clutter, single quotation marks have been used throughout. As for transliterations, Guénon was more concerned with phonetic fidelity than academic usage. The system adopted here reflects the views of scholars familiar both with the languages and Guénon's writings. Brackets indicate editorial insertions, or, within citations, Guénon's additions. Wherever possible, references have been updated, and English editions substituted.

The present translation is based on the work of Henry Fohr, edited by his son Samuel Fohr. The entire text was checked for accuracy and further revised by Patrick Moore and Marie Hansen. For help with selected chapters and proofreading thanks go to Alvin Moore, Jr., John Riess, and John Champoux, and, for final reviews, to, Brian and Michelle Latham, Benjamin Hardman, Allan Dewar, and John Ahmed Herlihy. A special debt of thanks is owed to Cecil Bethell, who revised and proofread the text at several stages and provided the index. Cover design by Michael Buchino and Gray Henry, based on a drawing of a Mycenaean Kylix from the Late Hellenic period, by Guénon's friend and collaborator Ananda K. Coomaraswamy..

THE WORKS
OF RENÉ GUÉNON

FOREWORD

PERHAPS IN ANTICIPATION of his approaching end, in the months immediately preceding his death René Guénon gave us some instruction regarding the handling of his work when he was gone. In letters dated August 30 and September 24, 1950, he ex-pressed, among other things, the desire that the articles he had not yet incorporated into his existing books should be collected into further volumes. 'There would only be,' he wrote,

> the difficulty of knowing in what way to arrange them so as to form collections that are as coherent as possible, which at present I am quite incapable of saying myself. . . . If I had an opportunity to undertake this, which unfortunately I find increasing doubtful, I would above all prefer to put together one or two collections of articles on symbolism and perhaps also a companion volume to *Aperçus sur l'Initiation* [published in English as *Perspectives on Initiation*], for it seems to me that there will soon be enough articles touching on that subject to make up a second volume.

The present work fulfills Guénon's wish, and we have chosen it to inaugurate the series of posthumous volumes because it could be more quickly reworked into its final form than the works on symbolism that Guénon originally envisaged, and also because the subject treated seemed to us to have a more immediate interest.

We must now say a few words regarding the composition of the present work. As we saw above, Guénon left no instructions regarding the distribution of the material to be published and so we had to assume that responsibility ourselves. The material we are presenting is entirely and exclusively from Guénon's pen. We have made no additions, modifications, or deletions except in those very rare cases necessitated by the presentation in one volume of isolated articles whose order of publication, often motivated by some then current circumstance, does not exactly coincide with the order that seemed to us most logical and to correspond best to the development of the author's thought. Regarding this order, we owe the reader some explanation.

In *Perspectives on Initiation*, Guénon applied himself to the task of defining the nature of initiation, which is essentially the transmission by appropriate rites of a spiritual influence intended to permit the being that is today a man to attain the spiritual state designated by the different traditions as the 'edenic state', and then to rise to the higher states of the being, and finally to obtain what can be called either 'Deliverance' or the state of 'Supreme Identity'. Guénon specified the conditions of initiation and the characteristics of the organizations entitled to transmit it, and in doing so noted on the one hand the distinction to be made between initiatic knowledge and profane culture, and on the other the no less important difference between the initiatic way and the mystical way.

The present work clarifies, completes, and illumines the above in several ways. The articles of which it is composed fall readily into four parts.

In the first part, Guénon considers the mental and psychological obstacles that may block comprehension of the initiatic point of view and the search for initiation. These are: belief in the possibility of 'popularizing' all knowledge; confusion between metaphysics and dialectics, which is its necessary and imperfect expression; fear; and concern about public opinion.

The second part clarifies and develops several very important points regarding the nature of initiation and certain of the conditions for its pursuit. In *Perspectives on Initiation*, the author had stated rather than demonstrated the necessity of an initiatic attachment. This demonstration is the aim of the first chapter of this second part, which also considers the case where the initiation is obtained outside the ordinary and normal means. The following chapter clearly differentiates the strictly spiritual influence from the psychic influence that is in a way 'clothes' it. Having made these points, Guénon then tackles a question he had previously not thought necessary to treat separately because it seemed to him to have been resolved in advance by his previous work as a whole: the necessity of a traditional exoterism for anyone aspiring to initiation.

This chapter finds a natural complement in the study on 'Salvation and Deliverance', which is the metaphysical 'justification' of exoterism. Directly related to the preceding subject, chapters 9, 10, and 11 show how 'ordinary life' can be 'sacralized' in such a way as to lose all its 'profane' character and to allow the individual a continual participation in Tradition, which is one of the conditions required for passage from virtual to effective initiation. But it must be recognized that in the Western world, even among representatives of the religious spirit still existing therein, there is a tendency toward an increasingly accentuated 'secularization' of social life, which betokens a disquieting loss of vitality in the Christian tradition. It is of course not impossible for a Westerner to seek a path to initiatic realization in a foreign tradition, and chapter 12 shows under what conditions what is commonly called a 'conversion' can be considered legitimate. Nevertheless passage to a foreign tradition is acceptable only if it is independent of any concern with 'estheticism' and 'exoticism', and the author points out that there are Westerners who, because of their special psychic constitution, will never be able to cease being so, and who would do much better to remain so definitely and entirely.

However, the former must stay away from all forms of pseudo-esoterism, whether of the occultists and Theosophists, or of those perhaps more seductive fantasies which, claiming to spring from an authentic Christianity, would particularly seem to have the aim of giving an apparent satisfaction to those Christians who find they cannot be content with the current exoteric teaching (chapter 14). In chapter 15, Guénon shows the inanity of the reproach of 'intellectual pride' so often levelled in certain religious circles against esoterism. Finally, this second part ends with some further points concerning the essential differences between initiatic and mystic realization.

With respect to *Perspectives on Initiation*, the subjects treated in part three are entirely new, and mainly involve the method and different paths to initiatic realization, as well as the question of the 'spiritual master'. The chapter 'Collective Initiatic Work and Spiritual "Presence"' is particularly important for those who cling to what still subsists of craft initiation in the Western world. Here the author shows that the presence of a human Master in such organizations is not as necessary as it is in other forms of initiation.

The last and in many respects the most important part, considers certain degrees of that spiritual realization which everything preceding it aims to make more easily understandable, and, to a certain degree, more easily accessible (chapters 26 to 29). The last three chapters, finally, which are truly the key both to *Perspectives on Initiation* and to the present book, provide a metaphysical exposition that allows an intellectual comprehension of the possibility of a total spiritual realization starting from our corporeal state, a realization that belonged by nature and function to the Divine Messengers called by the various traditions Prophet, Rasūl, Bodhisattva, and Avatāra.

In order to facilitate understanding of chapters 5 and 28, we thought it useful to reproduce in an appendix the texts recommended by the author relative to the Afrād and the Malāmatiyah, which designate degrees of effective initiation in Islamic esoterism.

JEAN REYOR

1

AGAINST
POPULARIZATION

PERHAPS THE MOST DIFFICULT THING in the world to bear is the
foolishness of a great number, and even the majority of men, especially in our time, a foolishness which grows ever greater in the
measure that the intellectual decline characteristic of the last cyclic
period becomes more general and accentuated. To this must be
joined ignorance, or more precisely a certain kind of ignorance that
is closely linked to it, one wholly unconscious of itself and asserting
itself all the more audaciously in the degree that it knows and
understands less, and as a result is an irremediable evil for those
afflicted by it.[1] Foolishness and ignorance can in short be united
under the common name of incomprehension; but it must be
understood that to endure this incomprehension in no way implies
that one must make any concessions to it, nor even abstain from
correcting the errors it gives rise to and doing all that is possible to
prevent it from spreading, which, moreover, is very often a most
unpleasant task, especially when the obstinacy of some people
obliges one to repeat many times what normally it should suffice to
say only once. This obstinacy which one thus comes up against is,
furthermore, not always exempt from bad faith; and, to speak the
truth, bad faith itself strongly implies a narrowness of view which is

---

1. In the Islamic tradition, *haqīqatu-zakāh* (the 'truth' of almsgiving) in its
inward and most real aspect consists in bearing human foolishness and ignorance
(haqīqah here is opposed to *muzāherah*, which is only the outward manifestation or
the accomplishment of the precept taken in its strictly literal sense). This naturally
arises from the virtue of 'patience' *(as-ṣabr)*, to which a very special importance is
attached, as is proved by the fact that it is mentioned 72 times in the Koran.

after all only the result of a more or less complete incomprehension; thus real incomprehension and bad faith, or stupidity and malice, intermingle in such a way that it is sometimes very difficult to determine the part each plays.

In speaking of concessions made to incomprehension, we are thinking especially of popularization in all its forms: can wishing to 'put within the reach of everyone' truths of any sort—or what at least are considered to be truths—'available to everyone', when this 'everyone' necessarily includes a great majority of the foolish and ignorant, really be anything other than this? Moreover, popularization proceeds from an eminently profane solicitude, and just as with any propaganda, it presupposes a certain degree of incomprehension on the part of those who indulge in it, no doubt relatively less than in the 'general public' to which it is addressed, but all the greater to the extent that what they thus claim to expound exceeds this public's mental level. This is why the drawbacks of popularization are more limited when what it attempts to diffuse is likewise wholly profane, like modern philosophical and scientific conceptions which, even as to those portions of truth they may happen to possess, certainly contain nothing profound or transcendent. This is moreover the most frequent case, since it is especially these things that interest the 'general public' due to the education that it has received, and this is also what most easily gives it the agreeable illusion of a 'knowledge' acquired at little cost. The popularizer always distorts things by simplification, and also by affirming peremptorily what the experts themselves regard as but mere hypotheses; but after all, in taking such an attitude he only continues the methods used in the rudimentary education that is imposed on everyone in the modern world and which, basically, is itself nothing but popularization, in a sense perhaps the worst popularization of all, for it gives the mentality of those who receive it a 'scientistic' imprint of which few are later able to rid themselves, and which the work of the popularizers properly so called only maintains and further reinforces, which attenuates their responsibility to a degree.

There is at present another sort of popularization which, although reaching a more restricted public, seems to present more serious dangers if only because of the confusions it can intentionally or unintentionally provoke, and which aims at things that by their nature ought most of all to be sheltered from such attempts; we mean traditional doctrines and, more particularly, Eastern doctrines. To tell the truth, the occultists and Theosophists have already attempted something of this sort, but have succeeded only in producing gross counterfeits. The attempts we now have in mind take on a more serious appearance, a more 'respectable' appearance we might say, which can overawe many people who would not have been seduced by distortions that are too obviously caricatures. Moreover, there is a distinction to make among popularizers with regard to their intentions if not to the results they achieve. Naturally, they all equally wish to spread the ideas they expound as widely as possible, but they can be moved by very different motives. On one hand, there are propagandists whose sincerity is certainly not in doubt but whose very attitude proves that their doctrinal comprehension does not go very far; what is more, even within the limits of what they understand, the needs of propaganda necessarily lead them to accommodate the mentality of those they address, which, especially when it is a question of an 'average' Western public, can only be to the detriment of the truth; the most curious thing is that this is such a necessity for them that it would be wholly unjust to accuse them of intentionally altering this truth. On the other hand, there are those who, at heart, are only indifferently interested in doctrines but who, having seen the widespread success of these things and hoping to profit from this 'fashion', have made a veritable commercial enterprise of it. Such people are much more 'eclectic' than the former and spread indiscriminately whatever seems to satisfy the taste of a certain 'clientele', which is obviously their principal concern even when they feel obliged to exhibit some claim to 'spirituality'. Of course, we do not wish to mention any names, but we think that many of our readers could themselves easily find examples of either case; and we are not speaking of mere charlatans as are found especially among the pseudo-esoterists, who knowingly deceive the public by presenting their own inventions under the label of doctrines about which they are almost wholly ignorant, thus further augmenting the mental confusion of this unfortunate public.

What is most troubling in all of this, besides the false or 'simplistic' ideas of traditional doctrines that are spread in this way, is that so many people do not even know how to distinguish between the work of these popularizers of every kind and an exposition made without any concern of pleasing the public or of putting it within their reach. They put everything on the same level and go so far as to attribute the same intentions to everything, even what is really furthest from them. This is stupidity pure and simple, but sometimes also bad faith, or more likely a mixture of both. To take an example that concerns us directly: after we have on every occasion clearly explained why and for what reasons we are resolutely opposed to all propaganda as well as to all popularization, and seeing that we have so often protested against the assertions of certain people who, despite this, still attribute propagandist motives to us, how is it still possible to think that these people or others like them are really acting in good faith when we see them indefinitely repeating the same calumny? Even though lacking any comprehension of the doctrines in question, if they at least had the smallest sense of logic, we would ask them to tell us what interest we could have in seeking to convince anyone whatsoever of the truth of this or that idea, and we are very sure that they would never find an answer to this question that would be to the slightest degree plausible. Indeed, among the propagandists and popularizers, some are this way because of a misplaced sentimentality, others because they find therein some material profit; but it is only too evident from the way in which we have explained doctrines that neither one nor the other of these two motives enters in the least into our work, and even if it be supposed that we ever had the intention of creating any sort of propaganda, we would then have necessarily adopted an attitude wholly contrary to the rigorous doctrinal strictness that we have constantly maintained. We do not wish to dwell further on this, but having for some time perceived from various quarters a strange recrudescence of the most unjust and most unjustifiable attacks, it seemed to us necessary, at the risk of drawing upon ourselves the reproach of repeating ourselves too often, to rectify things once more.

2

METAPHYSICS
AND DIALECTIC

WE RECENTLY LEARNED of an article that seems to deserve some attention because certain of the misapprehensions it evinces have been taken so far.[1] We were of course amused to read that those 'who have some experience of metaphysical knowledge' (among whom the author obviously places himself even while, with a remarkable impudence, denying us the privilege, as if he could possibly know!) will find nothing in our work but 'remarkably precise conceptual distinctions', that is, distinctions of a 'purely dialectical order', and 'representations that may serve as useful pre-liminaries, but that from the practical and methodological point of view do not advance one step beyond the realm of words toward the universal.' But we greatly fear that our contemporaries, so accustomed to stopping at external appearances, will commit similar errors: when we see them falling into error regarding traditional authorities such as Shankarāchārya for example, there is assuredly no reason for surprise that they do the same with regard to us, taking the 'husk' for the 'kernel'. However this may be, we would like to know how truth of any order whatsoever could be expressed without the use of words (excepting the case of purely symbolic figures, which are not under discussion here) and without a 'dialectical' form—in short,

---

1. Massimo Scaligero, *Esoterismo moderno: l'opera e il pensiero de René Guénon*, in the first issue of the new Italian journal *Imperium* (May, 1950). The expression 'modern esoterism' is itself already rather significant because it is a self-contradictory statement, and then again because there is quite obviously nothing 'modern' about our work, which is on the contrary and in every respect the very opposite of the modern spirit.

those discursive forms imposed by the very requirements of all human language—and also, given the subject under discussion, how any verbal explanation, whether written or oral, could be more than a 'useful preliminary'. It seems however that we have sufficiently stressed the essentially preparatory character of all theoretical knowledge, which is obviously the only knowledge that can be attained through a study of such explanations; but this is not at all to say that, in this respect and within these limits, it is not rigorously indispensable for all those who then wish to go further. And to avoid any misunderstanding let us immediately add that, contrary to what is said regarding a passage from our *Perspectives on Initiation*, we have never had the intention of saying anything about either our own 'inner experience', which is of no concern or interest to anyone, or anyone else's, since it is always something strictly incommunicable by its very nature.

Fundamentally, the author scarcely seems to understand what we mean by the term 'metaphysical', and even less what we mean by 'pure intellectuality', the 'transcendent' character of which he would like to deny, thus betraying the common confusion between intellect and reason, an error not unrelated to another he commits concerning the role of 'dialectic' in our writings (and, we could also say, in any writing concerned with this same realm). This is all too obvious when he asserts that 'the ultimate meaning of our work,' about which he speaks with an assurance that his incomprehension scarcely warrants, resides in a 'mental transparency, not recognized as such and with limits that are still "human", which we see at work when we take this transparency for effective initiation.' Faced with such assertions, we must once again repeat as clearly as possible that there is absolutely no difference between pure and transcendent intellectual knowledge (which, as such and contrary rational knowledge, has nothing 'mental' or 'human' about it), that is to say effective and not merely theoretical metaphysical knowledge, and initiatic realization, any more than between pure intellectuality and true spirituality.

This explains why the author considered it necessary to speak out, and even with some vehemence, about our 'thought', that is, about something which strictly speaking ought to be considered as non-existent, or at least ought to count for nothing when applied to our work, since it is not at all what we have put into the latter, which is exclusively an exposition of traditional data—only the expression being our own; this data, furthermore, is not the product of any kind of 'thought' whatsoever, by very reason of its traditional character, which essentially implies a supra-individual and 'non-human' origin. His error in this regard appears most clearly when he claims that we have 'mentally rejoined' the idea of the Infinite, which moreover is an impossibility; we have not in fact 'rejoined' it mentally or otherwise, for this idea (and again, this word can only be used in such cases if we rid it of the exclusively 'psychological' meaning currently ascribed to it) can only be grasped directly by an immediate intuition that belongs, we repeat, to the domain of pure intellectuality; all the rest are but means intended to prepare for this intuition those capable of it. It must be understood that as long as they are only 'thinking' through these means they will achieve no effective results, any more than someone who reasons or reflects on what are commonly called the 'proofs of the existence of God' will attain an effective knowledge of Divinity by this means alone. What it is necessary to know is that 'concepts' as such, and above all 'abstractions', do not interest us in the least (it goes without saying that this 'us' includes all who, like ourselves, adopt a strictly and integrally traditional point of view), and we willingly leave all these mental elaborations to philosophers and other 'thinkers'.[2] But when obliged to explain matters of an altogether different order, and especially in a Western language, we fail to see how one can avoid using words that in the majority of cases in fact only express simple concepts in current usage, since there are no others at our disposal;[3] if some are incapable of understanding the transposition that must be

2. For us, the very type of the 'thinker', in the proper sense of the word, is Descartes; whoever is simply that and nothing more will inevitably become a 'rationalist', since he is incapable of passing beyond the exercise of the purely individual and human faculties and is hence necessarily unaware of anything beyond their reach, which means that he can only be 'agnostic' regarding everything pertaining to the metaphysical and transcendent realm.

3. We need only except those words stemming from traditional terminology, in which case it is naturally enough to restore their original meaning.

effectuated in such a case in order to fathom the 'ultimate meaning', there is unfortunately nothing we can do about it. As for trying to discover in our work traces of the 'limits of our own knowledge', this is a waste of time, for, aside from this having nothing to do with 'us', our explanations are strictly impersonal by the very fact that they refer exclusively to truths of a traditional order; and, if we have not always succeeded in making this characteristic perfectly obvious, this should be ascribed rather to difficulties of expression.[4] This reminds us only too well of those who suppose that anyone who intentionally refrains from speaking about a thing is either ignorant of it, or does not understand it!

As for 'esoteric dialectic', this expression is acceptable only if one means by it dialectic in the service of esoterism as the external means used to communicate what can be expressed verbally, and always with the reservation that such an expression is necessarily inadequate, especially in the purely metaphysical order, by the very fact that it is formulated in 'human' terms. Dialectic is after all nothing but the use or practical application of logic;[5] now it hardly needs pointing out that the moment one wishes to say something it becomes necessary to conform to the laws of logic, which certainly does not mean that in themselves the truths to be expressed are dependent on these laws, any more than the fact that a draftsman is obliged to sketch a picture of a three-dimensional object on a two-dimensional surface thereby proves his ignorance of the existence of the third dimension. Logic does in fact dominate everything pertaining to reason, and, as its name indicates, this is its proper domain; but on the other hand everything of the supra-individual—and therefore supra-rational—order by this very fact obviously escapes that domain, for the superior could not be subservient to

---

4. In this respect, we have always regretted that the habits of our times have not permitted us to publish our works in the strictest anonymity, which, if nothing else, would have forestalled the writing of much nonsense and spared us the trouble of taking it up and correcting it.

5. We are of course taking 'dialectic' strictly in its original sense—the sense it had, for example, for Plato and Aristotle—without being in the least concerned about the special meanings attributed to it nowadays, which are derived more or less directly from Hegel's philosophy.

the inferior. Regarding truths of this order, logic can therefore only intervene in an incidental way, and their expression in discursive, or 'dialectical' mode is a kind of 'descent' to the individual level, failing which these truths would remain totally incommunicable.[6]

With singular inconsistency the author, even while reproaching us—through pure and simple incomprehension moreover—for stopping at the 'mental' level without realizing it, seems particularly embarrassed by the fact that we speak of the 'renunciation of the mental'. What he says on this subject is quite confused, but at bottom he seems unwilling to admit that the limits of individuality can be transcended, and that, as regards realization, for him everything is restricted (if we may express it so) to a sort of 'exaltation' of these limits, since he claims that 'the individual, by itself, tends to rediscover its original source,' which is precisely an impossibility for the individual as such since it obviously cannot surpass itself by its own means; and if this source were of an individual order, it would still be something very relative. If the being which is a human individual were truly nothing more than a being in a certain state of manifestation, there would be no way for him to emerge from the conditions of this state, and as long as he has not effectively emerged from it, that is, as long as he is still only an individual according to appearances (and we must not forget that for his present consciousness these appearances are confounded with reality itself, since they are all that he can attain of it), all that is necessary to enable him to go beyond them can only present itself as 'external',[7] for he has not yet

6. We shall not dwell on the reproach addressed to us that we speak 'as if transcendence and so-called external reality were separate from each other'; if the author knew what we have stated about 'descending realization'—or if he had understood it—he would certainly have dispensed with this criticism. This does not in any case alter the fact that this separation really exists 'in its own order', which is that of contingent existence, and that it ceases only for the one who has passed beyond this existence and is definitively free of its limiting conditions; whatever he may think, it is always important to know how to situate each thing in its rightful place, and at its proper degree of reality, and these are surely not distinctions of a 'purely dialectical order'!

7. It hardly seems necessary to remind the reader here that initiation naturally takes the aspirant as he is in his present state, in order to give him the means for transcending it, which is why such means may at first seem 'external'.

arrived at the stage where such distinctions as 'interior' and 'exterior' cease to be valid. Every conception that tends to deny these incontestable truths is nothing but a manifestation of modern individualism, whatever illusions those who hold to them may entertain in this regard;[8] and in the present instance the final conclusions, which are in fact equivalent to a negation of tradition and initiation under the pretext of rejecting all recourse to 'exterior' means of realization, show only too well that this is indeed so.

The author's conclusions now remain to be examined, and here there is at least one passage we must cite in its entirety: 'In the interior constitution of modern man there is a fracture that makes tradition appear to be an external collection of doctrines and rites, and not a supra-human current of life into which he might plunge himself in order to revive; in modern man lives the error that separates the transcendent world from that of the senses, so that he perceives the latter as deprived of the Divine; hence re-union or reintegration cannot come about through an initiatic form that antedates the time in which such an error became an accomplished fact.' We, too, are altogether of the opinion that this is indeed a most serious error, and also that this error, which properly speaking constitutes the profane point of view, is so characteristic of the modern spirit itself as to be truly inseparable from it, to the extent that, for those dominated by this spirit, there is no hope of freeing themselves from it. It is obvious that from the initiatic point of view this error is an insurmountable 'disqualification', which is why 'modern man' is really unfit to receive an initiation, or at least to attain to effective initiation; but we should add that there are exceptions, because in spite of everything even in the West today there are men who, by their 'interior constitution', are not 'modern men' but are capable of grasping the essence of tradition and do not accept this profane error as a *fait accompli*; and it is to these that we have always intended to address ourselves exclusively. But this is not all, for the author next falls into a curious contradiction, for he seems to want to present as 'progress' what he first recognized as error. Let us again quote his own words:

---

8. At present, many people sincerely believe themselves to be 'anti-modern', and yet are deeply affected by the influence of the modern spirit, which moreover is merely one of many examples of the confusion that reigns everywhere in our time.

To hypnotize men with the mirage of tradition and of an 'orthodox' organization to transmit initiation is in effect to paralyze that possibility of liberation and the conquest of liberty that for present-day man lies strictly in the fact that he has attained the ultimate degree of knowledge, that he has become conscious even to the point that the gods, the oracles, the myths, and the initiatic transmissions are no longer effective.

This is assuredly a strange misunderstanding of the real situation, for never has man been further than at present from the 'ultimate degree of knowledge', unless this be understood in the descending direction, and if he has really arrived at the point where all the things enumerated above no longer have an effect on him, it is not because he has climbed too high, but on the contrary because he has fallen too low, as is shown moreover by the fact that their many more or less crude counterfeits are quite effective in unbalancing him further. There is much talk about 'autonomy', the 'conquest of liberty', and so forth, always understood in a purely individualistic sense, but it is forgotten, or rather, remains un-known, that true liberation is only possible through emancipation from the limits inherent to the individual condition; one no longer wishes to hear of regular initiatic transmission or of traditional orthodox organizations, but what of the altogether comparable case of a man who, on the point of drowning, refuses the help offered him by a rescuer because it is 'external'? Whether we like it or not, the truth is—and this has nothing to do with any 'dialectic' whatsoever—that outside of an affiliation with a traditional organization, there is no initiation, and that without first being initiated, no metaphysical realization is possible; these are neither 'mirages' and 'ideal' illusions, nor vain 'speculations of thought', but entirely positive realities. Doubtless our opponent will argue that anything we say remains in the 'realm of words'; by the very nature of things, this is only too evident, and is equally true of what he says, but with one essential difference: however convinced he himself may be to the contrary, his words, for whoever understands their 'ultimate meaning', reflect nothing but the mental attitude of a profane person; and we ask him to believe that this is not meant as an insult on our part, but is merely the 'technical' expression of a simple fact.

3

THE MALADY
OF ANGUISH

THESE DAYS it is the fashion in certain circles to speak of 'meta-physical anxiety', and even of 'metaphysical anguish'. These patently absurd expressions give further proof of the mental disorder of our time; but, as always in such a case, there may be some interest in trying to find out precisely what lies behind these errors and what exactly such an abuse of language implies. It is clear enough that those who speak in this way do not have the slightest notion of what metaphysics really is. But one may still wonder why they wish to transpose these terms anxiety and anguish into whatever notion they have of this domain—of which they are ignorant—rather than any others that would be neither more nor less out of place. No doubt, the first or most immediate reason for this lies in the fact that these words represent certain sentiments particularly charac-teristic of the present age; and the predominance they have acquired today is moreover quite comprehensible, and could even be consid-ered legitimate in a certain sense if it were limited to the order of contingencies, for it is manifestly only too well justified by the present state of disequilibrium and instability of all things, a state which continues to worsen and is certainly not calculated to give a feeling of security to those who live in such a troubled world. If there is something morbid in these sentiments, it is that the state through which they are occasioned and maintained is itself abnor-mal and disordered; but all this, which amounts to no more than a simple explanation of fact, does not sufficiently take into account the intrusion of these same sentiments into the intellectual order, or at least into what lays claim to its place among our contemporaries;

this intrusion shows that the evil runs much deeper, and that there must be something in it related to the whole of the mental deviation of the modern world.

In this connection we may note first of all that the perpetual restlessness of the moderns is nothing other than one form of the need for agitation that we have often denounced, a need that in the mental order takes the form of research for its own sake, that is, research which, rather than leading to knowledge as it normally should, is pursued indefinitely and leads nowhere, and which moreover is undertaken without any intention of attaining truth, something in which so many of our contemporaries do not even believe. We admit that a certain anxiety may have its legitimate place at the starting-point of any inquiry as a motive inciting that very inquiry, for it goes without saying that if man were satisfied with his state of ignorance, he would remain in it indefinitely and never seek to escape it; but even so, it would be better to give such mental anxiety another name: in reality it is nothing other than the 'wonder' that according to Aristotle is the beginning of knowledge, and which of course has nothing in common with the purely practical needs to which the 'empiricists' and 'pragmatists' attribute the origin of all human knowledge. But in any case, whether one calls it anxiety or wonder it is something that could have no raison d'être nor subsist in any way once the inquiry has attained its goal, that is, once the knowledge in question has been attained—whatever order of knowledge is involved moreover; and its complete and definitive disappearance is all the more necessary when it is a question of knowledge par excellence, that is, knowledge of the metaphysical domain. One can thus see in the idea of an anxiety that has no end, and hence does not serve to draw man out of his ignorance, the mark of a sort of 'agnosticism', which may be more or less unconscious as the case may be, but which is no less real for all that. Whether one likes it or not, to speak of metaphysical 'anxiety' is basically equivalent either to denying metaphysical knowledge itself, or at the very least to declaring one's powerlessness to obtain it, which in practical terms amounts to no great difference. And when this 'agnosticism' is truly unconscious it is usually accompanied by an illusion that consists of mistaking for metaphysics something that is not only no such thing but that is not even to any degree a valid knowledge, even of a relative order. By this we mean the 'pseudo-metaphysics' of modern philosophers, which in effect is incapable of dispelling the slightest anxiety by the very fact that it is not a true knowledge, and which on the contrary cannot but increase the intellectual disorder and confusion of ideas in those who take it seriously, thereby rendering their ignorance all the more incurable. From this, as from every other point of view, false knowledge is certainly worse than simple unsophisticated ignorance.

As we have said, some people do not confine themselves to speaking of 'anxiety', but even go so far as to speak of 'anguish', which is more serious still, and expresses an attitude still more clearly anti-metaphysical, if that is possible; the two sentiments moreover are more or less connected in that both are rooted in ignorance. Anguish indeed is only an extreme and, so to speak, 'chronic' form of fear; now man is naturally inclined to fear what he does not know or understand, and this fear becomes an obstacle preventing him from conquering his ignorance, for it leads him to turn away from the object in whose presence he feels fear and to which he attributes its cause, whereas in reality that cause may perhaps reside only in himself; moreover, this negative reaction is only too often followed by a veritable hatred with respect to the unknown, especially if the person in question labors more or less confusedly under the impression that this unknown is something that exceeds his present possibilities of comprehension. If however the ignorance can be dispelled, the fear will immediately vanish by that very fact, as in the well-known example of the rope mistaken for a serpent; fear, and hence anguish, which is only one of its particular forms, is therefore incompatible with knowledge, and if it advances to such a point that it is truly invincible, knowledge will have been rendered impossible, even in the absence of any other hindrance inherent in the nature of the individual. In this sense one can thus speak, not of a 'metaphysical anguish', but on the contrary of an 'anti-metaphysical anguish' playing in a way the role of a veritable 'guardian of the threshold'—to use to a Hermetic expression— and forbidding man all access to the domain of metaphysical knowledge.

It is still necessary to explain more completely how fear results from ignorance, especially since we have recently come across a quite astonishing error on this subject: we have seen the origin of fear attributed to a feeling of isolation, and this in an exposition based on the Vedantic doctrine, whereas this latter expressly teaches, on the contrary, that fear is due to the feeling of duality; and indeed, if a man were truly alone, of what could he be afraid? It will perhaps be said that he may be afraid of something to be found within himself, but even this implies that in his present condition there are within him elements that escape his own understanding and are consequently a non-unified multiplicity; moreover, whether he is isolated or not changes nothing and in no way enters into such a case. On the other hand, one cannot validly invoke, in favor of this explanation by isolation, the instinctive fear of the dark that is felt by most people, especially children; in reality this fear is due to the idea that darkness may conceal things that one cannot see and that are therefore not known and for that very reason frightening; if, however, the darkness were considered as empty of all unknown presences, the fear would be without object and therefore would not arise. The truth is that the being experiencing fear seeks to isolate itself, but precisely in order to escape the fear; it adopts a negative attitude and 'withdraws', as if to avoid any possible contact with what it fears, whence undoubtedly arise the sensation of cold and other physiological symptoms that usually accompany fear. But this sort of unthinking defense is in any case ineffectual, for it is quite evident that, whatever a being may do, it cannot really isolate itself from the circumstances in which it is placed by the very conditions of its contingent existence, and that, so long as it considers itself surrounded by an 'external world', it is impossible that it find complete refuge from the latter. Fear can only be caused by the existence of other beings, which, insofar as they are other, constitute this 'external world', or other elements that, although incorporated in the being itself, are no less foreign and 'external' to his present consciousness; but the 'other' as such exists only by virtue of ignorance, since all consciousness essentially implies an identification. One can therefore say that the more a being knows, the less the 'other' or 'external' exists for it, and that in the same measure the possibility of fear, an altogether negative possibility moreover, is likewise abolished for him, and, finally, that the state of absolute 'solitude' (*kaivalya*), which is beyond contingency, is a state of pure impassibility. Incidentally, let us note in this regard that the 'ataraxy' of the Stoics represents only a deformed conception of such a state, for it claims to apply to a being that in reality is still subject to contingencies, which is contradictory. To try to treat exterior things as indifferent— to the extent one can in the individual condition—may constitute a kind of preparatory exercise with a view to 'deliverance', but nothing more, since for the being that is truly 'delivered' there are no 'exterior' things; in short, such an exercise could be regarded as equivalent to what, in initiatic 'trials', expresses in one form or another the need to conquer fear at the outset in order to attain knowledge, which will in turn render that fear impossible because there will then no longer be anything by which the person could be affected; and it is obvious that one must take care not to confuse the preliminaries of initiation with its final result.

Another observation, admittedly secondary but nonetheless not without interest, is that the sensation of cold and the exterior symptoms to which we alluded just now are also produced even without the one who experiences them being consciously afraid properly speaking, in cases where psychic influences of the most inferior order manifest themselves, as for example in spiritualist seances and in the phenomena of 'haunting'. Here again it is a case of the same subconscious and almost 'organic' defense in the presence of something hostile and at the same time unknown, at least to the ordinary man, who effectively knows only what is susceptible of being grasped by the senses, that is, only things of the corporeal domain. The 'panic terrors' which occur without any apparent cause are also due to the presence of various influences that do not belong to the perceptible order; moreover, they are collective, which again contradicts the explanation of fear through isolation; and in this case it is not necessarily a question of hostile influences or of the inferior order, for it may even happen that a spiritual influence—and not merely a psychic one—provokes a terror of this kind among the 'profane', who perceive it vaguely without knowing anything of its nature. An examination of these facts, which in short are not abnormal, despite common opinion, only further confirms that fear is indeed really caused by ignorance, and this is why we thought it well to note them in passing.

Returning to the essential point, we can now say that those who speak of 'metaphysical anguish' in the first place show thereby their total ignorance of metaphysics; furthermore, their very attitude renders this ignorance invincible, all the more so as anguish is not a simple momentary feeling of fear, but a fear become in a way permanent, installed in the very 'psychism' of the being, and that is why one can consider it a true 'malady': so long as it cannot be overcome it properly constitutes—as do all other serious defects of a psychic order—a 'disqualification' with respect to metaphysical knowledge. On the other hand, knowledge is the sole definitive remedy against anguish, as well as against fear in all its forms, and against simple anxiety, for these feelings are only the consequences or products of ignorance, and consequently, as soon as knowledge has been attained, it destroys them entirely at their very root and renders them henceforth impossible, whereas without it, even if they are momentarily put aside, they can always reappear under the pressure of circumstances. If it is a question of knowledge par excellence, this effect will necessarily have repercussions in all the various inferior domains, and thus such feelings will also disappear with regard to the most contingent things; indeed, how could they affect one who, seeing all things in their principle, knows that no matter what the appearances may be, they are ultimately only elements of the total order? What is true here is likewise true of all the evils from which the modern world suffers: the true remedy can come only from above, that is, from a restoration of pure intellectuality; as long as one seeks to remedy them from below, that is, resting content to oppose contingencies with other contingencies, all one's efforts will be vain and ineffectual—but who will prove able to understand this while there is still time?

4

CUSTOM
VERSUS TRADITION

WE HAVE REPEATEDLY DENOUNCED the strange confusion that
the moderns constantly make between tradition and custom;
indeed, our contemporaries are quite apt to give the name 'tradition' to all sorts of things that are really only customs, and often customs that are altogether insignificant and sometimes of very recent
invention. Thus it is enough that some profane festival—established
by anyone at all—simply endure a few years in order to be qualified
as 'traditional'. This abuse of language is evidently due to modern
man's ignorance of everything traditional in the true sense of the
word; but one can also detect in this a manifestation of that spirit of
'counterfeit' to which we have drawn attention on so many other
occasions: where nothing traditional any longer remains, people
seek consciously or unconsciously to substitute for it a sort of parody that can so to speak fill—at least in outward appearance—the
void left by its absence. It is then not sufficient to say that custom
differs entirely from tradition, for the truth is that it is even in stark
contrast to it, and that in more than one way it facilitates the diffu-
sion and maintenance of the anti-traditional spirit.

What must be understood first and foremost is this: all that is of
the traditional order implies essentially a 'supra-human' element,
custom on the contrary being something purely human, whether by
degeneration or by its very origin. Indeed, two cases must here be
clearly distinguished. First there are things that might formerly have
had a deeper meaning or even a properly ritual character, but
which, having ceased to be integrated into a traditional whole, have
lost it entirely and so are now no more than a 'dead letter' and a

'superstition' in the etymological sense; and since their purpose is no longer understood, they are particularly likely to be deformed and to become tainted with extrinsic elements arising from mere individual or collective fantasy. This is generally the case with customs to which it is impossible to assign a definite origin, the least that can be said of them being that they bear witness to the loss of the traditional spirit, and that they may be more serious as a symptom of this loss than they are in respect of their own drawbacks. Nonetheless, they still present a double danger: on the one hand, people are thus led to repeat actions simply from habit, that is, in a wholly mechanical fashion and without any valid reason, a result all the more unfortunate in that such a 'passive' attitude predisposes them to accept all sorts of 'suggestions' without reaction; on the other hand, by assimilating tradition to merely mechanical actions, the adversaries of tradition are not slow to take advantage of it by turning it to ridicule, so that this confusion, which with certain people is not entirely involuntary, is used to create an obstacle to any possibility of restoring the traditional spirit.

The second case is that where one can properly speak of 'counterfeits'. The customs we have just mentioned are, despite everything, still vestiges of something that originally possessed a traditional character, and as such they might not yet seem sufficiently profane. Thus the attempt, at a later stage, to replace them as much as possible by other customs that are wholly invented, which will be accepted all the more easily as people are already accustomed to doing things without meaning. And it is here that the 'suggestion' to which we just alluded intervenes. When people have been diverted from the accomplishment of their traditional rites, it is still possible that they will sense what is lacking and feel the need to return to them; to prevent this, 'pseudo-rites' are given them, and even imposed upon them if occasion allows; and this simulation of rites is sometimes pushed so far that there is no difficulty in recognizing the formal and scarcely disguised intention of establishing a sort of 'counter-tradition'. In this same order there are also other customs that, while apparently less offensive, are really far from being so, by which we mean customs that affect the life of each individual in particular rather than that of the whole collectivity; their role is again to stifle any ritual or traditional activity by substituting for it a preoccupation—it would not be an exaggeration to say obsession—with a multitude of perfectly insignificant, if not completely absurd, things of which the very 'pettiness' powerfully contributes to the ruin of all intellectuality.

The dissolving character of custom can be discerned very clearly today in Eastern countries, for as concerns the West it has long since passed the stage where it was even conceivable that all human actions might have a traditional character; but where the idea of 'ordinary life' (understood in the profane sense that we have explained elsewhere) has not yet become general, one can as it were catch in the act the manner in which such a notion takes shape and the role played in this by the substitution of custom for tradition. It goes without saying that we are speaking of a mentality that, at least for the present,[1] is hardly that of most people of the East, and belongs only to those who can be said to be more or less 'modernized' or 'Westernized', the two words basically expressing one and the same thing: when someone acts in a way that he cannot justify except by declaring that 'it is the custom', one can be sure that one is dealing with an individual detached from his tradition and no longer capable of understanding it; not only does he no longer accomplish its essential rites, but if he does keep some of its secondary 'observances', this is solely 'by custom' and for purely human reasons, among which concern for 'opinion' holds a preponderant place; and above all he will never be found wanting in the scrupulous observance of a host of those invented customs of which we were just speaking, customs that are in no way different from the silliness that constitutes the 'good manners' of modern Westerners, and that are sometimes pure and simple imitations of them.

What is perhaps most striking in these wholly profane customs, whether of the East or the West, is the incredible 'pettiness' we have already mentioned; it seems that they aim at nothing more than

---

1. These words were written almost fifty years ago. Today the ratio of modernists to traditionalists is very likely reversed, even in the East. The reader should note that by 'Easterners' Guénon means 'people of the East' and not only the so-called yellow race. ED.

directing all attention, not only to things that are entirely exterior and emptied of all meaning, but even to the very details of these things, to what is most banal and limited, which is obviously one of the best ways that exist to bring about a veritable intellectual atrophy in those who submit to it, and in the West what is called the 'worldly' mentality is the best example. Those in whom such preoccupations come to predominate, even without reaching this extreme degree, are only too manifestly incapable of conceiving any reality of a profound order; there is an incompatibility here so evident that it would be useless to dwell upon it further, and it is also clear that such people find themselves enclosed thenceforth in the circle of 'ordinary life', which is nothing, precisely, but a thick fabric of outward appearances like those on which they have been 'trained' to exclusively exercise all their mental activity. For them one might say that the world has lost all its 'transparency', for they no longer see in it anything that could be a sign or an expression of higher truths, and even if one were to speak to them of the inner meaning of things, not only would they fail to understand, but they would immediately begin to wonder what their peers might think or say of them if by chance they were to admit such a viewpoint, and even more conform their lives to it!

It is indeed the fear of 'opinion' that more than anything else allows custom to impose itself as it does and to take on the character of a veritable obsession: man can never act without some motive, legitimate or illegitimate, and when there can no longer exist any valid motive, as is the case here since we are speaking of actions that truly have no significance, one must then be found in an order that is as basely contingent and as deprived of all effective importance as is that to which these actions themselves belong. It might be objected that for this to be possible an opinion must already have been formed about the customs in question; but in fact it is enough that they be established in a very restricted milieu, even if at first merely as a 'fashion', for this factor to come into play. From this point, having become fixed by the very fact that no one dares any longer abstain from observing them, they can thereafter spread gradually, and correlatively what was initially only the opinion of a few ends by becoming what is called 'public opinion'. It could be said that respect for custom as such is fundamentally nothing other than respect for human stupidity, for in such a case this is what is naturally expressed in public opinion; moreover, 'doing as everyone else does'—to use the current expression—which for some seems to take the place of sufficient reason in all their actions, is necessarily to assimilate oneself to the vulgar and to endeavor to become wholly indistinguishable from them; it surely would be difficult to imagine anything more base and also more contrary to the traditional attitude, according to which each person must constantly strive to raise himself in the full measure of his possibilities, rather than sink down to the sort of intellectual nullity represented by a life wholly absorbed in the observation of the silliest customs, all for puerile fear of being judged unfavorably by whomsoever may happen along, that is to say by the foolish and the ignorant.[2]

It is said in traditional Arab countries that in the most ancient times men were distinguished from one another only by their knowledge; later, birth and descent were considered; later still, wealth became a mark of superiority; and finally, in the last times, men are judged solely by outward appearance. It is easy to see that this is an exact description of the successive predominance, in descending order, of the respective points of view of the four castes, or, if one prefers, of the natural divisions to which these correspond. Now custom incontestably belongs to the domain of those purely outward appearances behind which nothing is concealed: to observe custom in order to fall in line with opinion that honors such appearances only is therefore properly the action of a Shūdra.

2. If this was true when Guénon wrote fifty years ago, how much more true is it today, when the mass media and the world-wide advertising industry have made a quasi-science out of profiting from customs and public opinion. ED.

5

INITIATIC
AFFILIATION

MOST OF OUR CONTEMPORARIES, at least in the West, find certain matters so hard to understand that we are obliged to return to them repeatedly; and quite often these matters, which are at the root of all that is related to the traditional point of view in general or more especially to the esoteric and initiatic point of view in particular, are also of an order that ought normally to be regarded as rather elementary. Such for example is the question of the role and inherent efficacy of rites; and perhaps it is at least in part because of its rather close involvement with rites that the question of the need for initiatic affiliation seems to be in the same situation. Indeed, when one understands that initiation consists essentially in the transmission of a certain spiritual influence, and that this transmission can only be operated by means of a rite, which is precisely what effectuates the affiliation one to an organization that as its chief function conserves and communicates this influence, it does seem that there should no longer be any difficulty in this respect, for transmission and affiliation are fundamentally only the two inverse aspects of one and the same thing, according to whether it is envisaged as descending or ascending the initiatic 'chain'. Recently however we have had occasion to ascertain that this difficulty exists even for some who in fact have such an affiliation; this may seem rather astonishing, but we doubtless see here one result of the 'speculative' diminishment that the organization to which they belong has undergone, for it is obvious for anyone who confines himself to this single 'speculative' point of view, questions of this order, as well as all those that might properly be called 'technical', will only appear in a very indirect and distant perspective, and it is also clear that by this very fact their fundamental importance risks being more or less completely misunderstood. We might even say that such an example enables us to measure the distance separating 'virtual' from 'effective' initiation; not of course that the former can be regarded as negligible, for quite the contrary, it is this that constitutes initiation properly speaking, the indispensable 'beginning' (*initium*) that carries with it the possibility of all later developments. But we have to recognize that especially under present conditions, it is very far indeed from this virtual initiation to the slightest hint of realization. However this may be, we think we have already sufficiently ex-plained the need for initiatic affiliation,[1] but in the face of certain questions still being asked on this topic it will be useful to add a few points of detail to complement what we have already said.

We must first of all set aside the objection that some might be tempted to draw from the fact that the neophyte in no way experiences the spiritual influence at the actual moment of its reception; to tell the truth, this case is quite comparable to that of certain rites of an exoteric order, such, for example, as the religious rites of ordination, where a spiritual influence is also transmitted, and, at least in a general way, is no longer experienced either—which does not prevent it from being truly present and conferring upon those who receive it certain aptitudes that they would not have possessed without it. But in the initiatic order, we must go further; in a way it would be contradictory for the neophyte to be aware of the transmitted influence, since with respect to this influence as well as by definition he is still in a purely potential and 'non-developed' state, whereas the capacity to experience it would on the contrary necessarily imply a certain degree of development or actualization; and this is why we have just said that one must begin with a *virtual* initiation. But in the exoteric domain there is in fact no disadvantage in not having any conscious awareness of the influence received, even indirectly and in its effects, since in this domain it is not a matter of obtaining an effective spiritual development as a result of the effected transmission; on the other hand, it is an altogether different matter when it is a question of initiation, and hence the interior

1. See *Perspectives on Initiation*, especially chaps. 5 and 8.

work of the initiate, for ultimately the effects of this work should be felt, and this is precisely what constitutes the passage to effective initiation, at whatever degree it may be envisaged. This is at least what ought to take place normally if the initiation is to yield the results rightly expected from it. It is true that in most cases initiation remains forever virtual, which amounts to saying that the above-mentioned effects remain in a latent state indefinitely; but if this is the case, it is nonetheless an anomaly from a strictly initiatic point of view, and due only to certain contingent circumstances,[2] as, for instance, an initiate's insufficient qualifications (that is, the limitation of those possibilities which he bears within himself, and for which nothing external can make up), or again the state of imperfection or degeneration to which certain initiatic organizations are reduced at the present time, and which prevents them from furnishing sufficient support for the attainment of effective initiation, so that even the existence of such an initiation is unsuspected by those who might otherwise be qualified for it, although these organizations do remain capable of conferring a virtual initiation, that is, of assuring the initial transmission of a spiritual influence to those who possess the minimum of the indispensable qualifications.

Incidentally, and before passing to another aspect of the question, we should add that, as we have already expressly noted, this transmission does not and cannot have anything 'magical' about it for the very reason that it is essentially a matter of a spiritual influence, whereas everything of a magical order is concerned exclusively with the manipulation of psychic influences. Even if it happens that the spiritual influence is accompanied secondarily by certain psychic influences, this changes nothing, for it amounts to no more than a purely accidental result, due only to the correspondence that always necessarily obtains between different orders of reality; in all cases, initiatic rites do not act on or by means of these psychic influences, but stem solely from spiritual influences, and precisely insofar as they are initiatic, could not have any raison d'être outside of

---

2. One could say in a general way moreover that in the conditions of an age like ours it is almost always the truly normal case that from the traditional point of view appears as the exception.

the latter. The same is also true moreover in the exoteric domain concerning religious rites;[3] and regarding these as well as initiatic rites, whatever differences there may be between spiritual influences, either in themselves or with respect to the various ends to which they are directed, it is still properly a matter of spiritual influences. This suffices to show that they have nothing in common with magic, which is only a secondary traditional science of an altogether contingent and even of a very inferior order, and which is, we repeat, entirely foreign to everything that has to do with the spiritual domain.

We now come to what seems the most important point, one that touches most closely on the very root of the question, which, seen from this angle, might be formulated thus: nothing can be separated from the Principle, for if it were it would truly be without existence or reality, even in the smallest degree; how then can one speak of an affiliation, whatever may be the intermediaries by which it is effected, for ultimately this could only be conceived of as a link to the Principle itself, which, to take the word in its literal meaning, seems to imply the reestablishment of a link that had been broken? A question of this type is quite similar to another that has also been asked: Why do we need to make an effort to attain Deliverance, since the 'Self' (*Ātmā*) is immutable and remains always the same, and could not in any way be modified or affected by anything whatsoever? Those who raise such questions show that they have stopped at a much too exclusively theoretical and thereby one-sided view of things, or else that they have confused two points of view which, however, are clearly distinct, although complementary to each other in a certain sense—the principial point of view and that of manifested beings. Assuredly, from the metaphysical point of view one could if need be confine oneself to the principial aspect only and as it were neglect all the rest; but the properly initiatic point of view, on the contrary, must start from conditions that are

---

3. It goes without saying that the same holds true for exoteric rites in traditions other than those clothed in a religious form; if we speak more particularly of religious rites here, it is because, in this domain, they represent the most generally known case in the West.

those of manifested beings here and now, and more precisely, of human individuals as such, the very conditions, that is, from which it would have them liberate themselves; thus it must necessarily take into consideration—and this is what distinguishes this point of view from that of pure meta-physics—what might be called a 'state of fact', and in some way link it to the principial order. To avoid any ambiguity on this point we should say this: it is evident that in the Principle nothing could ever be subject to change, and so it is not the 'Self' that must be liberated, since it is never 'conditioned' or subject to any limitation, but rather the 'ego', and it can only be liberated by dissipating the illusion that makes it seem separate from the 'Self'. Similarly, it is not really the link with the Principle that must be reestablished, since it always exists and cannot cease to exist,[4] but for the manifested being, it is the effective consciousness of this link that has to be realized; and, in view of the present condition of humanity, there are no other possible means for this than those provided by initiation.

Hence one can understand that the necessity for an initiatic affiliation is not one of principle but only of fact, though one that is nonetheless rigorously indispensable in our present state and which we are consequently obliged to take as a starting-point. Besides, for the men of primordial times initiation would have been useless and even inconceivable, since spiritual development in all its degrees was accomplished among them in an altogether natural and spontaneous way by reason of their proximity to the Principle; but as a result of the 'descent' that has occurred since then, in conformity with the inevitable process of all cosmic manifestation, the conditions of the cyclic period in which we find ourselves at present are altogether different, and this is why the restoration of the possibilities of the primordial state is the first of the goals that initiation sets for itself.[5] It is therefore in taking account of these conditions such as they are

---

4. This link is basically none other than the *Sūtrātmā* of the Hindu tradition, which we have mentioned in other studies.

5. On initiation considered in connection with the 'lesser mysteries' as enabling the accomplishment of a 're-ascent' of the cycle by successive stages back to the primordial state, cf. *Perspectives on Initiation*, chap. 40.

in fact that we must affirm the necessity of an initiatic affiliation, and not in a general way and without further qualification as to the conditions of the age or, even more, of the world concerned. In this connection we would call attention more especially to what we have said elsewhere about the possibility that living beings might be born of themselves, without parents;[6] this 'spontaneous generation' is indeed a possibility in principle, and we can very well conceive a world where it would actually be so; but this is not an actual possibility in our world, at least, to be more precise, in its present state. It is the same for the attainment of certain spiritual states, which moreover is also a kind of 'birth',[7] and this comparison seems both the most exact and the best suited to help us understand what is involved. In the same order of ideas, we will also say this: in the present state of our world, the earth is unable to produce a plant of itself and spontaneously, except from a seed deriving necessarily from a pre-existing plant;[8] nevertheless the former case must have obtained at one time, for otherwise there could have been no beginning, although at present this possibility is no longer among those susceptible of manifestation. In the conditions in which we now in fact exist, no one can reap without first having sown, and this is just as true spiritually as it is materially; now, the seed that must be planted in our being in order to make possible our subsequent spiritual development is precisely the influence which, in a state of virtuality and 'envelopment' exactly comparable to that of a plant seed,[9] is communicated to us by initiation.[10]

6. *Perspectives on Initiation*, chap. 4.

7. In this regard there is hardly need to recall everything we have said elsewhere on initiation considered as a 'second birth'; moreover, this manner of envisaging things is common to all traditional forms without exception.

8. Let us point out, without being able to stress the point just now, that this is not unrelated to the grains of wheat of Eleusis, or, in Masonry, to the password of the grade of Companion; the initiatic application is moreover obviously closely related to the idea of 'spiritual posterity'. In this respect it is perhaps not without interest to note also that the word 'neophyte' means literally 'new plant'.

9. It is not that the spiritual influence in itself can ever be in a state of potentiality, but that the neophyte receives it in a manner somehow proportioned to his own state.

10. We could even add that, by reason of the correspondence that obtains between the cosmic order and the human order, there can be between the two

At this point it will be profitable to point out an error of which several examples have turned up recently: some people believe that affiliation with an initiatic organization is in some way merely a first step 'toward initiation'. This would only be true on condition that we clearly specify that this is the case with effective initiation; but the people in question do not make any distinction between virtual initiation and effective initiation, and perhaps do not even have the faintest notion of such a distinction, which, however, is of the greatest importance and even, one might say, altogether essential; besides, it is quite possible that they have been more or less influenced by certain conceptions of occultist or Theosophist provenance concerning the 'great initiates' and other things of this kind, which are assuredly apt to cause or maintain many confusions. In any case, such people obviously forget that initiation is derived from *initium*, a word that properly means 'entrance' and 'beginning': it is the entrance into a way that will be traversed thereafter, or again the beginning of a new existence in the course of which possibilities of another order will be developed, possibilities beyond the narrow confines of the ordinary life. Understood in its strictest and most precise sense, initiation is in reality nothing other than the initial transmission of a spiritual influence in its seed state, or in other words, initiatic affiliation itself.

Recently, another question concerning initiatic affiliation has been raised, but to correctly assess its scope we should first of all say that it particularly concerns cases where initiation is obtained outside the ordinary and normal channels,[11] and it must be clearly understood above all that such cases are never anything but exceptional, and that they occur when certain circumstances render normal transmission impossible, since their raison d'être is precisely to

terms of comparison that we have just indicated not just a similarity, but a much closer and more direct relationship, of such a nature as to justify it even more completely; and from this we can begin to see that the biblical text in which fallen man is represented as condemned to being no longer able to harvest anything from the soil without hard labor (Gen. 3:17–19) may well correspond to a truth, even in its most literal sense.

11. The explanatory note added to a passage of *Pages dédiées à Mercure d'Abdul-Hādi* (*Études Traditionnelles*, August 1946, pp318–9) and reproduced in the appendix to the present volume refers to these cases.

substitute in some measure for that transmission. We say 'in some measure' because such a thing can only happen with individuals possessing qualifications far beyond the ordinary and aspirations strong enough to in a way attract to themselves the spiritual influence that they would not find if left to their own devices, and also because for such individuals it is even rarer still—for lack of the assistance provided by constant contact with a traditional organization—that the results obtained through such an initiation are anything but fragmentary and incomplete. This cannot be insisted on too much, and yet to speak of such a possibility is nevertheless perhaps still not entirely without danger, if only because too many people have a tendency to entertain illusions in this regard; let an event occur in their lives that is a little extraordinary—or so it seems to them—but that is really rather commonplace, and they interpret it as a sign that they have received this exceptional initiation; and present-day Westerners in particular are all too easily tempted to seize upon the flimsiest pretext of this kind in order to dispense with a regular affiliation, which is why we are quite justified in insisting that as long as this latter is not in fact impossible to obtain one should not expect to receive any other kind of initiation apart from it.

Another very important point is this: even in such a case, affiliation with an initiatic 'chain' and the transmission of a spiritual influence is always involved, whatever may otherwise be the means and modalities, which no doubt can differ greatly from what they are in normal cases, and may for example imply an activity outside of the ordinary conditions of time and place; but at any rate there is necessarily a real contact, which assuredly has nothing in common with 'visions' or reveries that arise only from the imagination.[12] In certain well-known cases, such as that of Jacob Boehme, to which we have alluded elsewhere,[13] this contact was established by an

12. It should be kept in mind further that when questions of an initiatic order are involved one cannot be too distrustful of the imagination; whatever has to do only with 'psychological' or 'subjective' illusions is completely worthless in this respect, and should not be allowed to intervene in any way or to any degree.

13. *Perspectives on Initiation*, chap. 10.

encounter with a mysterious personage who did not reappear thereafter; whoever this personage may have been,[14] what we have here is a perfectly 'positive' fact, and not simply a more or less vague and ambiguous 'sign' to be interpreted as one likes. But it is must be understood that an individual initiated by such means may not have any clear awareness of the true nature of what he has received or to what he has thus been affiliated. What is more, lacking 'instructions' that could enable him to gain some idea, however imprecise, on all of this, he himself may be quite incapable of explaining the matter; he may not even have heard of initiation, the word and the thing itself being totally unknown in his milieu, but this is basically of small concern and obviously does not in any way affect the reality of that initiation itself, provided we understand that this kind of initiation presents certain inevitable disadvantages with respect to normal initiation.[15]

Having said this, we now come to the question alluded to previously, for these few remarks enable us to answer it more easily: is it not possible that certain books, of which the contents are of an initiatic order, can, for particularly qualified individuals who study them with the requisite frame of mind, serve by themselves as vehicles for the transmission of a spiritual influence, so that in such an instance their reading would suffice, without there being any need for direct contact with a traditional 'chain', to confer on them an initiation of the type mentioned above? The impossibility of an initiation through books is yet again a point we thought we had sufficiently explained elsewhere, and we must admit that we had not anticipated that the reading of any books whatsoever could be envisaged as constituting one of those exceptional ways that sometimes replace the ordinary means of initiation. Besides, even outside

14. It may have been an instance, though certainly not necessarily so, of the appearance assumed by an 'adept' acting, as we were just saying, outside of the ordinary conditions of time and place. To better understand possibilities of this order, cf. *Perspectives on Initiation*, chap. 42.

15. Among other consequences, these disadvantages often give the initiate, especially as regards his manner of expression, a certain exterior resemblance to the mystics, which may even cause him to be taken as such by those who do not go to the heart of things, as was precisely the case with Jacob Boehme.

of those particular and special cases where it is properly a matter of the transmission of an initiatic influence, there is here something clearly opposed to the fact that an oral transmission is always and everywhere considered a necessary condition of true traditional teaching, so much so that putting this teaching in writing can never dispense with it;[16] and this because, to be really valid, its transmission implies the communicating of a 'vital' element as it were, for which books could not serve as a vehicle.[17] But what is perhaps most astonishing is that this question was raised in connection with a passage about 'bookish' studies (a passage in which we thought that matters were explained with sufficient clarity to preclude any misunderstanding), where we indicated that precisely those books having an initiatic content were apt to give rise to such misunderstandings;[18] and so it would not seem useless to return to this topic and to explain more completely what we had wanted to say.

It is obvious that there are many different ways of reading one and the same book, and that the results will vary accordingly; in the case of a tradition's sacred scriptures, for example, a person who is profane in the most complete sense of the word, such as the modern 'critic', will view it only as 'literature', from which he will only be able to derive that kind of exclusively verbal knowledge which constitutes pure and simple erudition, without the addition of any real comprehension of even the most exterior kind, since he does not know and does not even ask whether what he is reading is the

16. In a book the content itself, as a body of words and sentences expressing certain ideas, is therefore not the only thing that really matters from the traditional point of view.

17. It might be objected that according to some accounts referring especially to the Rosicrucian tradition, certain books were charged with influences by the authors themselves, which is indeed possible for a book as well as for any other object; but even admitting the reality of this fact, it could in any case only be a question of specific copies especially prepared to that end; moreover, each of these copies would have been destined exclusively for a given disciple, to whom it was directly entrusted, not to take the place of an initiation, which that disciple would have already received, but solely to furnish him with more effective help when, in the course of his personal work, he would use the contents of the book as a support for meditation.

18. *Perspectives on Initiation*, chap. 34.

expression of a truth; and this is the kind of knowledge that can be qualified as 'bookish' in the strictest sense of the term. Anyone affiliated to the tradition in question, even if he knows only its exoteric side, will already see something altogether different in its scriptures, although his comprehension may still be limited to the literal sense alone; but what he finds there will be incomparably more valuable for him than any erudition, and this remains equally true for those at the lowest level, who, through an incapacity to understand doctrinal truths, regard them simply as rules of conduct which at least enable them to participate in the tradition to the extent of their possibilities. And yet someone like the theologian who aims at assimilating the exoterism of the doctrine as completely as possible and is thus situated at a very much higher level, is still only concerned with the literal sense, and may not even suspect the existence of other more profound meanings—in short, those of esoterism—whereas on the contrary someone having no more than a theoretical grasp of esoterism will, with the help of certain commentaries or otherwise, be able to begin to perceive the plurality of meanings contained in the sacred texts, and hence be in a position to discern the 'spirit' hidden beneath the 'letter'; his comprehension therefore will be of a much more profound and lofty order than that which is aspired to by the most learned and accomplished of the exoterists. The study of such texts can then form an important part of the doctrinal preparation that normally must precede all realization; but if the one devoting himself to this does not also receive an initiation, he will always be left with an exclusively theoretical knowledge, no matter what predisposition he brings to it, which no amount of study will of itself enable him to surpass.

If instead of the sacred scriptures we consider certain writings of a properly initiatic character, as for example those of Shankarā-chārya or Muḥyi 'd-Dīn ibn al-'Arabī, we could, except on one point, say almost exactly the same thing, and so, to take one instance, the only gain that an orientalist could derive from reading them would be to know that such an author (indeed, they are for him 'authors' and nothing more) has said such or such a thing; furthermore if he wishes to express this material in his own words rather than resting content to repeat it verbatim by a simple act of memory, there is the greatest risk that he will deform it, since he has not assimilated its real meaning to any degree. This only differs from what we mentioned earlier in that there is no longer any reason to consider the case of the exoterist since these writings relate to the esoteric domain alone and as such are entirely beyond his competence; were he truly able to understand them, he would by that very fact already have crossed the boundary separating exoterism from esoterism, and then we would in fact be in the presence of a 'theoretical' esoterist, of whom we could only repeat unaltered what we have already said on this subject.

Nothing remains now but to focus on one last difference, which however is not the least important from our present point of view: this is the difference between the reading of one and the same book by both the 'theoretical' esoterist just mentioned (who, we will suppose, has not yet received any initiation) and by someone who already possesses an initiatic affiliation. The latter will naturally see in it things of the same order as the former, though perhaps more completely, and above all they will appear to him in a different light as it were; moreover, it goes without saying that as long as his is only a virtual initiation, he can do no more than simply pursue, to a more profound degree, a doctrinal preparation that had remained incomplete until then; but it is altogether different once he enters into the way of realization. For him the content of the book is then properly no more than a support for meditation, in the sense one might call 'ritual', and in exactly the same way as the various kinds of symbols he uses to assist and sustain his inner work; surely it would be inconceivable for traditional writings, which by their very nature are necessarily symbolic in the strictest sense of this term, not to play such a role as well. Beyond the 'letter', which has now as it were disappeared for him, he will truly see nothing but the 'spirit', and thus possibilities altogether different from those inherent in a simple theoretical understanding will be as open to him as when he meditates by concentrating on a *mantra* or a ritual *yantra*. But if this is so, it is only, we repeat, by virtue of the initiation received, which constitutes the necessary condition without which, whatever qualifications an individual might otherwise possess, there cannot be the slightest beginning of realization—which in short amounts simply to saying that every effective initiation necessarily presupposes a virtual initiation. And we can add further that if it happens that someone meditating on an initiatic piece of writing really enters into contact by its means with an influence emanating from the author thereof (which is in fact possible if the writing originates in a traditional form, and especially from the particular 'chain' to which he himself is attached), this too, far from taking the place of an initiatic affiliation, can on the contrary never be anything but a consequence of a prior affiliation. However we look at it then, there can be absolutely no initiation through books, but only, under certain circumstances, an initiatic use of books, which is obviously something altogether different. We hope that this time we have sufficiently stressed this point so that not even the slightest ambiguity remains, and that no one will continue to think that there might be something here which lends itself, even if only under exceptional circumstances, to dispensing with the need for an initiatic affiliation.

6

SPIRITUAL
INFLUENCES
AND 'EGREGORES'

In a review devoted to our *Perspectives on Initiation* we were recently a bit surprised to read the following statement, presented in such a way as to give the impression that it sums up what we ourselves said in that book: 'Certainly initiation dispenses with neither meditation nor study, but it places the adept on a particular plane; it puts him in contact with the egregore of an initiatic organization, which has itself emanated from the supreme egregore of a universal initiation, one and multiform.' We will not dwell on the abuse here of the word 'adept,' although, since we have explicitly denounced this usage when explaining the true meaning of the word, some astonishment is permitted; from initiation properly so called to the state of an adept, major or even minor, is a long way. But what is most important is this: since the review in question makes not the slightest allusion to the role of spiritual influences, it seems to labor under a rather grave error, which others may equally have committed despite all the care we have taken to explain things as clearly as possible, for it definitely seems that it is often very difficult to make oneself understood exactly. We think, therefore, that a restatement will not be without use; moreover, these precise details will provide a natural follow-up to those we made in our latest articles in response to different questions that we were asked on the subject of initiatic affiliation.

First of all, we must point out that we have never used the word 'egregore' to designate what could properly be called a 'collective entity'; the reason for this is that this term is wholly untraditional and only represents one of the many fantasies of modern occultist language. The first person to use it in this way was Eliphas Levi, and if our memory is exact, it was also he who, to justify this meaning, gave it an improbable Latin etymology, deriving it from *grex*, 'flock,' whereas the word is purely Greek and has never signified anything but 'watcher.' Moreover, this term is known to be found in the book of *Enoch* where it designates entities of a rather enigmatic character that, whatever they may be, seem to belong to the 'intermediary world'; this is all that they have in common with the collective entities to which the same name has been applied. These latter are in fact of an essentially psychic order, and it is above all this that makes the error we noted so serious, for the sentence we quoted appears in the final analysis to be a new example of the confusion of the psychic with the spiritual.

Indeed, we have spoken of these collective entities, and we think that we sufficiently explained their role when we wrote the following on the subject of traditional organizations, religious or otherwise, that belong to the domain that can be called exoteric in the widest sense of the word, in order to distinguish it from the initiatic domain:

> Each collectivity can thus be regarded as possessing a subtle force made up in a way of the contributions of all its members past and present, and which is consequently all the more considerable and able to produce greater effects as the collectivity is older and is composed of a greater number of members. It is evident, moreover, that this 'quantitative' consideration essentially indicates that it is a question of the individual domain, beyond which this force could not in any way intervene.[1]

In this connection we will recall that the collective, in its psychic as well as its corporeal aspects, is nothing but a simple extension of the individual, and thus has absolutely nothing transcendent with respect to it, as opposed to spiritual influences, which are of a wholly different order. To use the customary terms of geometrical

---

1. *Perspectives on Initiation*, chap. 24.

symbolism once again, the horizontal direction must not be confused with the vertical. This leads us incidentally to answer another question we have been asked, which is not unrelated to the question under discussion. It would be an error to consider as supra-individual the state that results from identification with a collective psychic entity of whatever kind, or indeed with any other psychic entity; participation in such a collective entity at any degree can be regarded, as it were, as constituting a sort of 'enlargement' of the individuality, but nothing more. Thus it is solely to obtain certain advantages of an individual order that the members of a collectivity can use the subtle force at its disposal, in conformity with the rules established to this end by the collectivity in question; and even if there is the additional intervention of a spiritual influence in obtaining these advantages, as happens particularly with religious collectivities, this spiritual influence no longer acts in its own domain, which is of a supra-individual order, and, as we have already said, must be seen as 'descending' into the individual domain and exercising its action there by means of the collective force which it takes as its support. This is why prayer, consciously or not, addresses itself most immediately to the collective entity, and it is only by the intermediary of this latter that it also addresses the spiritual influence that works through it. The conditions arranged for its efficacy by the religious organization cannot be explained otherwise.

The case is wholly different with initiatic organizations by the very fact that these, and these alone, have the essential goal of going beyond the individual domain, and that even what relates more directly to the development of the individuality constitutes in the final analysis only a preliminary stage for finally surpassing the limitations of that domain. It goes without saying that these organizations, like all the others, also include a psychic element that can play an effective role in certain respects, for example to establish a 'defense' toward the outer world and to protect members from various dangers arising from the latter, for it is evident that such results cannot be obtained by means of a spiritual order, but only by means that are as it were on the same level as those posed by the outer world; but this is something very secondary and purely contingent that has nothing to do with initiation itself. Initiation is entirely independent of the action of any psychic force since it consists strictly and essentially in the direct transmission of a spiritual influence that must produce effects whether immediate or deferred, that depend equally on the spiritual order itself, and not, as in the case discussed earlier, to a lower order; in this case, therefore, the spiritual influence no longer acts by the intermediary of a psychic element. Thus an initiatic organization as such must not be envisaged as a mere collectivity, for the collectivity can never provide that which enables it to fulfill the function that is its whole raison d'être. Since in the final analysis a collectivity is only a union of individuals, it cannot by itself produce anything of a supra-individual order, for the higher can never proceed from the lower. If affiliation with an initiatic organization can have effects of a supra-individual order, this is solely to the extent that the initiatic organization is the depository of something that is itself supra-individual and transcendent with respect to the collectivity, that is, of a spiritual influence, the conservation and transmission of which it must ensure without any discontinuity. Thus initiatic affiliation must not be thought of as affiliation with an 'egregore' or with any collective psychic entity, for this is only a completely accidental aspect in which initiatic organizations do not differ at all from exoteric organizations. What essentially constitutes the 'chain', let it be said again, is the uninterrupted transmission of the spiritual influence across successive generations.[2] Likewise, the link between the different initiatic forms is not a mere filiation of 'egregores', as one might be led to believe from the text which formed the starting-point of these reflections; in reality, it results from the presence in all these forms of one and the same spiritual influence, one as to its essence and as to the ends in view of which it acts, if not as to the more or less particular modalities by which it acts. And it is only as a result of this that, step by step and in different degrees, a communication, effective or virtual as the case may be, can be established with the supreme spiritual center.

---

2. We use the word 'generations' here not only in its outward and as it were 'material' meaning, but especially to allude to the character of 'second birth' inherent to every initiation.

We will add to these considerations another remark that also has its importance from the same point of view. When an initiatic organization finds itself in a more or less marked state of degeneration, although the spiritual influence always remains present, its action is necessarily diminished, while the psychic influences, on the contrary, can act in a more visible and sometimes almost independent fashion. The extreme case of this can be seen when an initiatic form has ceased to exist as such and the spiritual influence has been entirely withdrawn, leaving behind the psychic influences alone as harmful and even particularly dangerous residues, as we have explained elsewhere.[3] Of course, as long as initiation really exists, even if reduced to something purely virtual, things cannot go so far. But it remains true that a preponderance of psychic influences in an initiatic form constitutes an unfavorable sign as to its actual state, and this again shows how far from the truth those are who would relate initiation itself to influences of this order.

3. *The Reign of Quantity and the Signs of the Times*, chap. 27.

7

THE NECESSITY OF
TRADITIONAL
EXOTERISM

MANY PEOPLE SEEM to doubt whether it is really necessary for one who aspires to initiation to attach himself first of all to a traditional form of the exoteric order and fulfill all its prescriptions; moreover, this is indicative of a state of mind peculiar to the modern West, for reasons that are no doubt numerous. We will not undertake to ascertain how much of the responsibility for this lies with the very representatives of religious exoterism, whose exclusivism too often tends to deny more or less expressly all that passes beyond their domain; but this aspect of the question is not what interests us here, for what is more astonishing is that those who consider themselves qualified for initiation should display a basically equivalent incomprehension, although here it is applied in an inverse manner. It is indeed admissible that an exoterist be ignorant of esoterism, although such ignorance does not of course justify a negation of it, but what is inadmissible is that anyone with pretensions to esoterism should ignore exoterism, even if only in a practical way, for the 'greater' must necessarily comprehend the 'lesser'. Besides, this practical ignorance, consisting as it does of regarding participation in an exoteric tradition as useless or superfluous, would not be possible without a theoretical misunderstanding of this aspect of tradition; and it is this misunderstanding that makes the matter all the more serious, for it can be asked whether someone with such a misunderstanding, whatever his other possibilities may be, is really prepared to approach the initiatic and esoteric domain, and whether he ought not rather apply himself to better understanding the value and scope of exoterism before seeking to go further. In fact, there is manifest here an enfeeblement of the tra-ditional spirit understood in its general sense, and it should be obvious that it is this spirit that one must first integrally restore in oneself if one wishes thereafter to penetrate the profound meaning of tradition; the misunderstanding in question is fundamentally of the same order as that concerning the efficacy proper to rites, which is also so widespread in the contemporary West. We readily admit that the profane ambience in which many live renders the comprehension of these things more difficult; but it is precisely against the influence of this ambience that they must react in every regard, until they have succeeded in realizing the illegitimacy of the profane point of view itself—a matter to which we shall shortly return.

We have said that the state of mind we are denouncing here is peculiar to the West. Indeed, it could not exist in the East, first because of the persistence of the traditional spirit there, which still penetrates the entire social milieu,[1] and then also because where exoterism and esoterism are directly linked in the constitution of a traditional form[2] in such a way as to be as it were the two faces, exterior and interior, of one and the same thing, it is immediately comprehensible to everyone that one must first adhere to the exterior in order subsequently to be able to penetrate to the interior,[3] and that there can be no other way than this. This may appear less evident in the case—which actually occurs in the contemporary West—where one finds oneself in the presence of initiatic organizations with no

1. We speak here of the milieu taken as a whole and so need not take into account 'modernized'—or 'Westernized'—elements, which, however clamorous they may be, constitute in spite of everything only a small minority.

2. For ease of expression we use the two terms 'exoterism' and 'esoterism' in their widest sense and for ease of expression, which should cause no inconvenience, for it goes without saying that, even in a tradition where such a division is not formally established, there is necessarily always something that corresponds to both two points of view; in the present case, moreover, the link between them is all the more evident.

3. One can also say, according to a frequently employed symbolism, that the kernel can only be reached by way of the shell.

link to the whole of a definite traditional form; but then we can say that, in principle at least, they are by this very fact compatible with every exoterism, whatever it may be, although from the strictly initiatic point of view, which alone concerns us here to the exclusion of a consideration of contingent circumstances, these initiatic organizations are not really compatible with the absence of any traditional exoterism.

In order to explain things in the simplest way possible let us say first that one does not build upon the void, and wholly profane existence, that is, existence from which all traditional elements are excluded, is in this respect really only void and nothingness. If one wishes to construct a building one must first lay down the foundation, which provides the indispensable base upon which the whole edifice, including its loftiest parts, will rest—and this foundation remains, even when the building is completed. In the same way, adherence to an exoterism is a preliminary condition for coming to esoterism and furthermore one must not believe that this exoterism can be rejected once initiation has been obtained, any more than the foundation can be removed once the building has been constructed. Exoterism, far from being rejected, must in reality be 'transformed' in the measure corresponding to the degree attained by the initiate, for he becomes more and more qualified to understand the profound reasons for it; and as a result the doctrinal formulas and rites take on for him a significance much more genuinely important than they could have for the mere exoterist who in the end is by definition always restricted to the exterior appearance alone, that is, to what counts least with regard to the 'truth' of the tradition envisaged in its integrality.

Then also—and this brings us back to a consideration we alluded to above—whoever does not take part in any traditional exoterism by this very fact gives the purely profane outlook the greatest conceivable scope in his own individual existence; and in these conditions he must necessarily conform all his exterior activity to this outlook. At another level and with wider consequences this is the same error as that committed by the majority of those modern Westerners who believe themselves still 'religious' but make of religion something entirely apart, having no real contact with the rest of their lives. Such an error is moreover all the less excusable for one who wishes to place himself at the initiatic point of view than for one who keeps to the exoteric perspective; and in any case it is easily seen how far this is from corresponding to an integrally traditional conception. Basically, this amounts to admitting that outside or alongside the traditional domain there is a profane domain that is equally legitimate in its own order. Now, as we have often said before, there is really no profane realm to which some things belong by their very nature; there is only a profane point of view, which is merely the product of the spiritual degeneration of humanity, and which consequently is entirely illegitimate. In principle, then, one ought to make no concession to this point of view, but in the present Western environment this is assuredly very difficult to do in fact—and perhaps even impossible in certain cases and up to a certain point—for apart from very rare exceptions each individual is obliged by the necessity for social relationships to submit himself more or less to the conditions of 'ordinary' life, at least in appearance, which precisely is nothing other than the practical application of this profane point of view. But even if such concessions are indispensable in order to live in this environment, they should nevertheless be kept to a strict minimum by all those for whom tradition still has meaning, whereas they are on the contrary pushed to the utmost by those who claim to dispense with all exoterism, even if this is not their intention and even if they are only more or less unconsciously coming under the influence of the profane milieu. Such dispositions are certainly as unfavorable as can be to initiation, which has to do with a domain that exterior influences must normally not penetrate in any way. If, however, because of the anomalies inherent to the conditions of our age, those harboring this attitude are nonetheless able to receive a virtual initiation, we strongly doubt that it will be possible for them to go further and proceed to effective initiation so long as they voluntarily persist in this orientation.

8

SALVATION
AND DELIVERANCE

WE RECENTLY OBSERVED, not without some astonishment, that some of our readers still experience difficulty in understanding the essential difference between salvation and Deliverance. We have however already explained our position on this question many times, and in any case this ought to pose no problem for anyone possessing the idea of the multiple states of the being and, above all, that of the fundamental distinction between the 'ego' and the 'Self'.[1] It is therefore necessary to return to the subject in order to dispel definitively any possible misunderstanding and to leave no room for any objection.

In the present conditions of terrestrial humanity, it is evident that the great majority of men are wholly incapable of going beyond the

---

1. Another thing that, in truth, is much less surprising to us is the obstinate incomprehension of the orientalists in this regard, as in so many others. We recently saw a rather curious example of it: in a review of *Man and His Becoming according to the Vedānta*, one of them, noting with ill disguised bad humor our criticisms of his colleagues, mentions as something particularly shocking what we said about the 'constant confusion between salvation and Deliverance', and he appears indignant that we faulted a certain Indianist for having translated *Moksha* by 'salvation' from one end of his works to the other, without seeming even to suspect the mere possibility of an inexactness in this assimilation. Obviously it is wholly inconceivable to him that *Moksha* could be anything other than salvation! This aside, what is truly amusing is that the author of this review 'deplores' the fact that we have not adopted the orientalists' transcription, even though we expressly stated our reasons for this, and also that we did not include a bibliography of works by orientalists, as if they ought to have been 'authorities' for us and as if, from our point of view, we did not have the right purely and simply to ignore them. Such remarks give the correct measure of the comprehension of certain people.

limits of the individual condition, either during their lives or after leaving this world by bodily death, which in itself can change nothing about the spiritual level they possess at the moment it occurs.[2] Since this is so, exoterism in its broadest sense, that is to say the part of tradition addressed indiscriminately to all, can only offer them an end of a purely individual order, since any other would be entirely inaccessible to most of the adherents of the tradition, and it is precisely this end that constitutes salvation. It goes without saying that it is a long way from here to effective realization of a supra-individual though still conditioned state, not to mention Deliverance, which, as the achievement of the supreme and unconditioned state, truly has no common measure with any conditioned state whatsoever.[3] We will immediately add that if 'Paradise is a prison' for some, as we said earlier, this is precisely because the being that finds itself in the state to which this corresponds—that is, the being that has attained salvation—is still locked, even for an indefinite duration, in the limitations that define human individuality. This condition can only be a state of 'privation' for those who aspire to be freed from these limitations and whose degree of spiritual development renders them effectively capable of it even during their terrestrial life, although the others who do not themselves possess the possibility of going further can in no way feel this 'privation' as such.

One can thus ask the following question: even if the beings in this state are not conscious of its imperfection with respect to higher states, this imperfection nonetheless exist in reality; what advantage is there then in keeping these beings indefinitely in this state, since it

2. Many people seem to imagine that the sole fact of death can suffice to give a man intellectual or spiritual qualities that he never possessed while alive. This is a strange illusion, and we do not see what reasons could be invoked to give it the least appearance of justification.

3. Incidentally, we will explain that if we are accustomed to begin 'salvation' in the lower case and 'Deliverance' with a capital, this is to mark clearly that one is of the individual order and the other of a transcendent order, just as when we write 'ego' and 'Self'. This remark is meant to prevent anyone attributing to us intentions that are in no way ours, such as depreciating salvation in some way, when it is solely a matter of situating it as exactly as possible in the place that in fact belongs to it in total reality.

is the normal result of exoteric traditional observances? The truth is that there is a very great one, for being fixed thereby in the prolongations of the human state as long as this state itself subsists in manifestation—which is equivalent to perpetuity or an indefinite time—these beings will not be able to pass on to another individual state, which otherwise would necessarily be the only possibility open to them. But once again, why in this case is the continuation of the human state more favorable than the passage to another state? Here we must interpose a consideration of the central position occupied by man in the degree of existence to which he belongs, while all other beings in this state are more or less peripheral, their specific superiority or inferiority in relation to one another resulting directly from their greater or lesser distance from the center; and this determines the different measures of their participation, which is always only partial, in the possibilities that can only be expressed completely in and by man. But, when a being must pass to another individual state, nothing guarantees that there it will again occupy a central position relative to the possibilities of that state, as it does in its present state; on the contrary, there is even an incomparably greater probability that it will encounter one of the innumerable peripheral conditions comparable in our world to those of animals or even vegetables. One can immediately understand how serious a disadvantage this would be, especially from the point of view of the possibilities for spiritual development, even if, as would be normal to suppose, this new state envisaged in its entirety constituted a degree of existence higher than ours. This is why certain oriental texts say that 'human birth is difficult to obtain,' which of course applies equally to what corresponds to it in every other individual state; and this is also the reason why exoteric doctrines portray the 'second death' as a formidable and even sinister eventuality, this death being the dissolution of the psychic elements by which the being ceases to belong to the human state and thereby must necessarily and immediately be born into another state. It would be wholly different and even quite the contrary if this 'second death' gave access to a supra-individual state; but this is no longer the province of exoterism, which can and must consider only the most general case, while the exceptions are precisely what constitute the raison d'être of esoterism. Ordinary man, who cannot attain a supra-individual state, can if he attains salvation at least reach the end of the human cycle; he will thus escape the danger we have just mentioned and so will not lose the benefit of his human birth; on the contrary, he will preserve it in a definitive way, for to say salvation is to say preservation, and it is this that is of essential importance in such a case, for it is in this, but only in this, that salvation can be considered to bring the being closer to his ultimate destination, or, as improper as such a manner of speaking may be, to constitute in a certain sense progress toward Deliverance.

Moreover, one must take great care not to be led into error through certain apparent similarities of expression, for the same terms can have many meanings and be applied at very different levels according to whether it is a question of the exoteric or esoteric domain. Thus, when the mystics speak of 'union with God', what they mean by this can certainly not be assimilated in any way to *Yoga*; and this remark is particularly important because some people might perhaps be tempted to say: how can a being have a higher end than union with God? All depends on the sense in which one takes the word 'union'. In reality, the mystics, like all other exoterists, are concerned with nothing more or other than salvation, although what they have in view is, if one wishes, a higher modality of salvation, for it is inconceivable that there should not also be a hierarchy among 'saved' beings. In any case, since in mystical union individuality as such subsists, it can only be a wholly exterior and relative union, and it is quite evident that the mystics have never even conceived the possibility of the Supreme Identity; they stop short at 'vision', and the entire extent of the angelic worlds still separates them from Deliverance.

9

RITUAL AND MORAL
POINTS OF VIEW

As WE HAVE REMARKED ON VARIOUS OCCASIONS, similar phenomena can proceed from entirely different causes. This is why
phenomena in themselves, which are only outward appearances,
can never really constitute proof of the truth of any doctrine or the-
ory, contrary to the illusions of modern 'experimentalism' in this
regard. The same is true of human actions, which moreover are also
phenomena of a kind: the same actions, or to speak more exactly,
actions that are outwardly indistinguishable from one another, can
relate to very different intentions among those who perform them;
and more generally, two individuals can even act in similar ways
throughout almost all the circumstances of their lives even though
the points of view that regulate their conduct in reality have almost
nothing in common. Naturally, a superficial observer who limits
himself to what he sees and who goes no further than appearances
will never fail to let himself be deceived in this regard and will uni-
formly interpret the actions of all men in relation to his own point
of view. It is easy to understand that this can be the cause of many
errors, as in the case of men belonging to different civilizations for
example, or with historical facts dating from distant ages. A very
striking and as it were extreme example of this is provided us by
those of our contemporaries who, because 'economic' considerations in fact play a preponderant role for themselves, seek to
explain all of human history by appealing exclusively to matters of
this order, without even thinking to ask whether this has been true
in all times and places. This is an effect of the tendency, also to be
observed among psychologists, to believe that men are always and

everywhere the same, a tendency perhaps natural in a certain sense, but nonetheless unjustified, and we think one of which we cannot be too mistrustful.

There is another error of the same kind that risks, even more easily than the one we have just described, escaping the notice of many people and indeed of the great majority, because they are too accustomed to envisaging things in this manner, and also because, unlike the 'economic' illusion, it does not seem to be directly linked to any particular theories. This error consists in attributing the specifically moral point of view to all men without distinction, that is, in translating into 'moral' terms, with the special intentions these imply, every rule of action whatsoever, even when it belongs to civilizations completely different from theirs in every respect, simply because it is from this point of view that modern Westerners derive their own rule of action. Those who think in this way seem incapable of understanding that there are indeed other points of view that also can furnish such rules, and that, as we were just saying, the outward similarities that may exist in men's conduct in no way proves that it is always governed by the same point of view. Thus the precept to do or not to do something, which some may obey for reasons of the moral order, can be observed equally by others for wholly different reasons. It must not be concluded from this that in themselves and independently of their practical consequences, the viewpoints in question are all equivalent, far from it, for what could be called the 'quality' of the corresponding intentions varies to such a degree that there is, so to speak, no common measure between them; and this is more particularly true when comparing the moral point of view to the ritual point of view that belongs to integrally traditional civilizations.

According to the original meaning of the word itself, and as we have explained elsewhere, ritual action is what is accomplished 'in conformity with order'. It consequently implies an effective consciousness of this conformity, at least to some degree; and where tradition has not undergone any diminishment, every action whatsoever has a properly ritual character. It is important to note that this essentially presupposes the knowledge of the solidarity and correspondence that exist between the cosmic order and the human order; this knowledge, with the multiple applications deriving from it, exists in all traditions, whereas it has become completely foreign to the modern mentality, which sees nothing but fantastic 'speculations' in everything that does not fall within its crude and narrowly limited conception of what it calls 'reality'. For anyone not blinded by prejudice, it is easy to see the distance separating a consciousness of conformity with the universal order, and the participation of the individual in this order by virtue of that very conformity, from the mere 'moral conscience' that requires no intellectual comprehension and is guided by nothing except purely sentimental aspirations and tendencies, and what a profound degeneration in the general mentality of humanity is implied by the passage from the one to the other. Moreover, it goes without saying that this passage is not accomplished all at once and that there can be many intermediate degrees where the two corresponding points of view intermingle in different proportions. In fact, the ritual point of view always exists in every traditional form of necessity, but some traditional forms, such as those that are properly religious, give a greater or lesser part to the moral perspective alongside the ritual point of view, and we shall see the reason for this shortly. However this may be, once one finds oneself in the presence of the moral point of view in a civilization, one can say that it is no longer integrally traditional, whatever the appearances in other respects; or in other words, the appearance of this viewpoint can be considered to be linked in some way to that of the profane point of view.

This is not the place to examine the stages of this degeneration which leads finally to the modern world, to the complete disappearance of the traditional spirit, and thus to the invasion by the profane outlook of all domains without exception; we will only note that in the present order of things it is this last stage that is represented by the so-called 'independent' ethics which, whether they call themselves 'philosophical' or 'scientific' are really only a degeneration of religious ethics, that is to say, they are to this latter much as the profane sciences are to the traditional sciences. Naturally there are also corresponding degrees in the incomprehension of traditional realities and in the errors of interpretation to which they give rise; in this regard the lowest degree is held by the modern conceptions which, no longer content even to see in ritual prescriptions only ethical rules, and thus already misunderstanding their profound reason, go so far as to attribute to them vulgar preoccupations with hygiene or cleanliness; it is obvious indeed that, after this, incomprehension could hardly be pushed further!

There is another question that is more important for us at present: how could authentic traditional forms have conceded a place to the moral perspective, as we were just saying, even incorporating it as one of their constituent elements, instead of remaining at the pure ritual point of view? It was inevitable that this happen once the human mentality as a whole fell to a lower level in the descending course of the historical cycle; in order to direct men's actions efficaciously it is necessary to have recourse to means appropriate to their nature, and when this nature is mediocre, the means must also be so in a corresponding degree, for this is the only way to save those who can still be saved in such conditions. Once the majority of men are no longer capable of understanding the reasons for ritual action as such, in order that they should nonetheless continue to act in a still normal and 'regular' fashion, it is necessary to appeal to secondary motives, ethical or otherwise, but in any case of a much more relative and contingent—and, we might add, thereby lower—order than those inherent in the ritual point of view. In this there is really no deviation but only a necessary adaptation; the particular traditional forms must be adapted to the circumstances of time and place that determine the mentality of those to which they are addressed, since it is this that is the very reason for their diversity, especially regarding their most outward aspect which must be common to all without exception, and to which all rules of action naturally relate. As for those still capable of another order of comprehension, it is obviously their responsibility to effect the transposition by placing themselves at a higher and more profound point of view which always remains possible as long as the link with principles has not been broken, that is to say, as long as the traditional point of view itself continues to subsist; thus they need only consider ethics as a mere outward mode of expression that does not affect the very essence of things clothed by it. Thus, for example, there is surely as great a difference as possible between one who accomplishes actions for ethical reasons and one who accomplishes them in view of an effective spiritual development to which they can serve as preparation; their mode of acting is nonetheless the same, but their intentions are wholly different and in no way correspond to the same degree of comprehension. But it is only when morality has lost all traditional character that one can truly speak of deviation; emptied of all real meaning and no longer possessing anything that could legitimize its existence, this profane ethics is properly speaking nothing more than a 'residue' without value and a pure and simple superstition.

10

THE 'GLORIFICATION OF WORK'

IN OUR TIME it is fashionable to exalt work of whatever sort and no matter how it is accomplished, as if it had some superlative value in itself independently of any consideration of another order. This has been the subject of innumerable pronouncements as empty as they are pompous, not only in the profane world but, what is more serious, even in the initiatic organizations remaining in the West.[1] It is easy to understand that this way of envisaging things is directly linked to the exaggerated need for action that characterizes modern Westerners; work, at least when so considered, is obviously nothing but a form of action, and a form to which the 'moralist' prejudice is bound to attribute more importance than to any other because it more easily lends itself to being presented as a 'duty' for man and as ensuring his 'dignity'.[2] Added to this there is usually a clearly anti-traditional motive, namely the depreciation of contemplation, which is assimilated to idleness, whereas on the contrary it is really the highest activity conceivable, and whereas further, action separated from contemplation can only be blind and disordered.[3] All of

---

1. In Masonry the 'glorification of work' is notably the theme of the final part of initiation to the grade of Companion; and unfortunately, it is today generally understood in this wholly profane manner instead of being understood, as it ought to be, in the legitimate and truly traditional sense that we propose to describe in what follows.

2. Let us immediately say that between this modern conception of work and its traditional conception there is all the difference which exists in a general way between the moral viewpoint and the ritual viewpoint, as we explained above.

3. Here let us recall one of the applications of the fable of the blind man and the

this only too easily accounts for those who declare, no doubt sincerely, that 'their happiness lies in action' itself;[4] we would rather say in 'agitation', for once action is thus taken for an end in itself, whatever the 'moralist' pretexts invoked to justify it, it is truly nothing more than that.

Contrary to what the moderns think, any work that is done indiscriminately by anyone solely for the pleasure of acting or because of the need to 'earn one's living' hardly merits being exalted, and indeed it can only be regarded as something abnormal, opposed to the order that ought to regulate human institutions, to such a point that, in the conditions of our age, it only too often acquires a character that without any exaggeration qualifies as 'infra-human'. What our contemporaries seem to ignore completely is that work is not truly valid unless it conforms to the very nature of the being that accomplishes it and results therefrom in a spontaneous and necessary way, as it were, so that it is no more than the means for that nature to realize itself as perfectly as possible. This in sum is the very notion of *svadharma*, which is the true foundation of the caste system and which we have emphasized sufficiently on many other occasions, so that here we can content ourselves by recalling it without further discussion. In this connection one can also consider what Aristotle said about the accomplishment by each being of its 'proper activity', by which must be understood both the exercise of an activity in conformity to its nature and, as an immediate consequence of this activity, the passage from 'potency' to 'act' of the possibilities comprised in this nature. In other words, in order for work of any sort to be what it ought to be, it must above all correspond to a person's 'vocation' in the proper meaning of this word;[5] and when

paralytic, who represent respectively the active life and the contemplative life (cf. *Spiritual Authority and Temporal Power*, chap. 5).

4. We take this phrase from a commentary on Masonic ritual, which nonetheless is in many ways certainly not the worst, that is, not one most affected by infiltrations of the profane spirit.

5. On this point as on the other considerations that follow, we will refer to the numerous studies that A. K. Coomaraswamy devoted particularly to these questions for fuller explanations.

things are thus, the material profit that can legitimately be derived from it is only a wholly secondary and contingent, not to say negligible end compared to the higher end, which is the development and as it were the fulfillment 'in act' of the very nature of the human being.

It goes without saying that what we have just said constitutes one of the essential foundations of any craft initiation, for the corresponding 'vocation' is one of the requisite qualifications for such an initiation and is even, one might say, the first and most indispensable.[6] There is nonetheless one other thing that needs to be emphasized, particularly from the initiatic point of view, for it gives to work in its traditional understanding its deepest meaning and highest importance, going beyond a consideration of human nature alone to link it with the cosmic order itself, and through this, in the most direct way, to universal principles. In order to understand this, one can begin with the definition of art as the 'imitation of nature in its mode of operation,'[7] that is to say nature as cause (*Natura naturans*), and not as effect (*Natura naturata*). From the traditional point of view there is no distinction between art and craft, any more than between artist and artisan, and this also is a point that we have already had occasion to explain. All that is produced 'in conformity with order' thereby equally and by the same right merits consideration as a work of art.[8] All traditions insist on the analogy between human artisans and the divine Artisan, both operating 'by a word conceived in the intellect,' which, let us note in passing, marks as clearly as possible the role of contemplation as the preliminary and necessary condition to the production of any work of art; and this too is an essential difference from the profane conception of work, which, as we said above, reduces it purely and simply to action, and

6. Certain modern occupations, especially those that are purely mechanical and for which there cannot really be any question of 'vocation', and which consequently have in themselves an 'abnormal' character, cannot validly be the occasion for any initiation.

7. And not in its productions, as the partisans of a so-called 'realist' art imagine, which art is more exactly called 'naturalistic'.

8. It is hardly necessary to recall that this traditional notion of art has absolutely nothing in common with the 'esthetic' theories of the moderns.

which even tries to oppose it to contemplation. According to the Hindu scriptures, 'we must build as the *Devas* did in the beginning'; this, which naturally extends to the exercise of all crafts worthy of the name, implies that work has a properly ritual character, as moreover all things ought to have in a civilization that is integrally traditional; and this ritual character not only ensures that 'conformity to order' of which we have just spoken, but one can even say that it is truly one with this conformity itself.[9]

When the human artist thus imitates the operation of the divine Artist in his own particular domain, he participates to a corresponding measure in the very work of the divine Artist, and in a way that is all the more effective as he is the more conscious of that operation; and the more he realizes through his work the virtualities of his own nature, at the same time the more his resemblance to the divine Artist increases, and the more perfectly his works are integrated into the harmony of the Cosmos. One can see how far this is from the banalities our contemporaries are in the habit of pronouncing in the belief that they are praising work; but when work is all that it traditionally ought to be, and only then, it is in reality far above all that they are capable of conceiving. Thus we can conclude these few remarks, which could easily be developed almost indefinitely, by saying this: the 'glorification of work' indeed corresponds to a truth, and even to a profound truth; but the way in which modern people understand it is nothing but a deformed caricature and in a way even an inversion of the traditional notion. Work is not 'glorified' by vain discourse, something which does not even have a plausible meaning; but work itself is 'glorified', that is to say 'transformed', when, instead of being a mere profane activity, it constitutes a conscious and effective collaboration toward the realization of the plan of the 'Great Architect of the Universe'.

9. For all of this, see A.K. Coomaraswamy, 'Is Art a Superstition or a Way of Life?' in the collection entitled *Why Exhibit Works of Art?*

11

THE SACRED
AND THE PROFANE

WE HAVE OFTEN EXPLAINED that in an integrally traditional civilization every human activity, whatever it may be, possesses a sacred character, for by very definition tradition leaves nothing outside of itself; its applications thus extend to all things without exception in such a way that nothing can be considered indifferent or insignificant in regard to it, and such that whatever a man does, his participation in the tradition is constantly assured by his very actions. As soon as certain things are excluded from the traditional point of view or, what amounts to the same thing, are regarded as profane, this is a manifest sign that there has already been a degeneration entailing a weakening and attenuation of a tradition; in human history such a degeneration is naturally linked with the descending course of cyclic unfolding. Obviously there can be many different degrees, but, as a general rule, it can be said that today, even in civilizations that previously maintained the most clearly traditional character, a certain portion of daily life is always given over to the profane as a kind of forced concession to a mentality determined by the very conditions of the age. This is not to say however that a tradition can ever recognize the profane point of view as legitimate, since this would be tantamount to denying itself, at least partially and to the degree of latitude accorded to that point of view. Through all of its successive adaptations, tradition can only maintain in principle, if not in fact, that its own point of view is really valid for all things and includes them all equally.

Owing to its essentially anti-traditional spirit, modern Western civilization is unique in affirming the legitimacy of the profane as such and even in considering it 'progress' to include in it an ever-increasing portion of human activity. Indeed, this is so true that for the wholly modern spirit nothing exists but the profane, and all of its efforts ultimately tend finally to the negation or exclusion of the sacred. The relationships are here reversed: even an attenuated traditional civilization can only tolerate the existence of the profane point of view as an unavoidable evil, and endeavor to limit its consequences as much as possible; in modern civilization, on the contrary, it is the sacred that is tolerated, and only because it cannot destroy it at a single blow. While waiting for the complete realization of this 'ideal', it grants it a smaller and smaller role, taking the greatest care to isolate all the rest behind an impenetrable barrier.

The passage from one to another of these opposed attitudes implies the conviction that there is not only a profane point of view, but a profane domain, that is, that there are things that are profane in and of themselves, and according to their very nature, and not, as in reality, as a result of a certain mentality. This affirmation of a profane domain, which unjustifiably changes a simple state of fact into a state of law, is one of the fundamental postulates of the anti-traditional spirit, for it is only by first inculcating this false conception into the minds of the generality of men that it can hope gradually to achieve its goal, that is, the disappearance of the sacred, or in other terms, the eradication of tradition, even to its last vestiges. One need only look around to realize how far the modern spirit has succeeded in its self-appointed task. Even men who esteem themselves 'religious', that is, those in whom there still subsists more or less consciously something of the traditional spirit, only consider religion as occupying a place wholly apart among other things, indeed, a place so restricted that it exerts no effective influence on the rest of their lives, where they think and act exactly as the most completely irreligious of their contemporaries. What is most serious is that these men do not simply act this way because they feel obliged to do so by the constraints of the milieu in which they live, because they are in a situation that they can only deplore and from which they are unable to escape. Were this the case it would be admissible, for assuredly one cannot demand of everyone the courage necessary to react openly against the dominant tendencies of the age, which to be sure is not without danger in many respects. But, so far from this being the case, these men are affected by the modern spirit to such a point that like everyone else they regard the distinction and even the separation of the sacred from the profane as perfectly legitimate, and see in the traditional and normal structures of civilization nothing but a confusion of two different domains, a confusion that has been 'surpassed' and advantageously done away with by 'progress'!

There is still more. Such an attitude, barely conceivable on the part of men who call and believe themselves religious, is no longer only the attitude of the 'laity', for whom it could be attributed to a certain, partially excusable, ignorance; but this same attitude now appears to belong to an ever-growing number of the clergy, who do not seem to understand how contrary it is to tradition, and here we mean tradition as such, thus the one they represent as well as every other traditional form. And it has been pointed out to us that some go so far as to reproach the Eastern civilizations for having a social life still penetrated by the spiritual, seeing this as one of the principal causes of their supposed inferiority to Western civilization! Furthermore, we notice a strange contradiction here: the clergy with the most modern tendencies show themselves more preoccupied with social action than with doctrine; however, since they accept and even approve the 'laicization' of society, why do they intervene in that domain? It cannot be a legitimate and desirable attempt to reintroduce some modicum of the traditional spirit into it, since they believe this spirit should remain completely foreign to the activities of the social' order. This intervention is thus completely incomprehensible, unless we admit that there is something profoundly illogical in their mentality, as is undeniably the case with many of our contemporaries. Be that as it may, we have here a most disquieting symptom. When the authentic representatives of a tradition reach the point where their way of thinking does not differ appreciably from that of their adversaries, we are forced to wonder what degree of vitality remains in this tradition in its present state, and since it is a question of the tradition of the Western world, what are its chances for rectification under these conditions, at least if we confine ourselves to the exoteric domain and do not envisage any other order of possibilities?

12

CONVERSIONS

THE WORD 'CONVERSION' can be taken in two totally different senses. Its original meaning corresponds to the Greek term *metanoia*, which properly expresses a change of *nous*, or, as A.K. Coomaraswamy has said, an 'intellectual metamorphosis'. This interior transformation, indicated moreover by the Latin etymology (*cum-vertere*), simultaneously implies both a 'gathering' or concentration of the powers of the being, and a certain 'return' by which the being passes from 'human thought' to 'divine comprehension'. *Metanoia* or 'conversion' is therefore the conscious passage of the ordinary and individual mind, normally turned toward sensible things, to its superior transposition, where it is identified with the *hēgemōn* of Plato or the *antaryāmī* of the Hindu tradition. It is obvious that this passage is a necessary phase in every process of spiritual development. It must be understood that this development is of a purely interior order, having absolutely nothing in common with any kind of exterior and contingent change, whether arising simply from the 'moral' domain, as is too often believed today (*metanoia* is even translated as 'repentance'), or from the religious and more generally exoteric domain.[1]

After the above explanations, and in order to avoid any confusion, we must now take up the common meaning of the word 'conversion', the meaning it bears constantly in contemporary language, where it designates only the exterior passage from one traditional form to another, whatever the reasons that determined the change, reasons usually completely contingent, sometimes lacking any real

---

1. On this subject, see A.K. Coomaraswamy, 'On Being in One's Right Mind' in *What is Civilization?* (Great Barrington, MA: Lindisfarne Press, 1989).

importance, and in any case having nothing to do with pure spirituality. Although without doubt more or less spontaneous conversions can sometimes occur, at least in appearance, they usually result from religious 'proselytism', and it goes without saying that all the objections which can be formulated against the value of this 'proselytism' apply equally to its results. In short, both the 'convertor' and the 'convertee' show the same incomprehension of the profound meaning of their traditions, and their respective attitudes show only too manifestly that their intellectual horizon is likewise limited to the viewpoint of the most exclusive exoterism.[2] Even aside from this reason of principle, but for others reasons too, we have little regard for 'converts' in general, not that their sincerity should be doubted *a priori* (for here we do not consider the all too frequent case of those motivated by some base material or sentimental interest, who really should be called 'pseudo-converts'), but first because they give proof at the very least of a rather unfortunate lack of mental stability, and then because they almost always have a tendency to the narrowest and most exaggerated 'sectarianism', either because of their own temperament, which has driven some to pass from one extreme to another with disconcerting ease, or simply as a means of deflecting the suspicions they fear in their new milieu. Basically, 'converts' are of little interest, at least for those who look at things without any prejudice of exoteric exclusiveness and have no taste for the study of various 'psychological' curiosities. For our part, we certainly prefer not to examine them too closely.

Having said this, we must turn to a point that we have been especially wanting to discuss. People often speak of 'conversions' very inappropriately and in cases where this word, understood in the sense just given above, could never be applied, that is, the case of those who, for reasons of an esoteric and initiatic order, adopt a traditional form different from that to which they would seem to be linked by their origin. This could be either because their native tradition furnished them with no possibility of an esoteric order, or

---

2. In principle, there is only one really legitimate conversion, the one that consists in the connection to a tradition, whatever it may be, on the part of someone who was previously lacking any traditional attachment.

simply because their chosen tradition, even in its exoteric form, gives them a foundation that is more appropriate to their nature, and consequently more favorable to their spiritual work. Whoever places himself at the esoteric point of view has this absolute right, against which all the arguments of the exoterists are of no avail, since by very definition this matter lies completely outside their competence. Contrary to what takes place in 'conversion', nothing here implies the attribution of the superiority of one traditional form over another. It is merely a question of what one might call reasons of spiritual expediency, which is altogether different from simple individual 'preference', and for which exterior considerations are completely insignificant. Moreover, it is of course understood that one who can legitimately act in this way must, since he is truly capable of placing himself at the esoteric point of view, be conscious, at least by virtue of a theoretical if not an effectively realized knowledge, of the essential unity of all traditions. This alone is sufficient to show that when the word 'conversion' is applied to such a case, it is meaningless and truly inconceivable. If it is asked why there are such cases, we reply that is due above all to the conditions of the present age in which, on the one hand, certain traditions have become incomplete 'from above', that is, from their esoteric side, the existence of which their 'official' representatives sometimes even go so far as to more or less formally deny; and on the other hand, it too often happens that someone is born into a milieu not in harmony with his own nature, and because not really suitable for him, does not allow his possibilities, especially of the intellectual and spiritual order, to develop in a normal manner. Certainly it is regrettable in more than one respect that things are this way, but these are the inevitable drawbacks of the present phase of the *Kali-Yuga*.

Besides the case of those who 'take up their abode' in a traditional form because it puts at their disposal the most adequate means for the interior work they have yet to accomplish, there is another that we must also mention. This is the case of men who, having reached a high degree of spiritual development, adopt outwardly one or another traditional form according to circumstances and for reasons of which they are the sole judges, especially since these reasons are generally those which necessarily escape the understanding of ordinary men. Because of the spiritual state they have reached, these men are beyond all forms, for whom they are only a matter of outward appearance, unable to affect or modify their inner reality in any way. Not only have they reached that understanding spoken of earlier, but they have fully realized, in its very principle, the fundamental unity of all traditions. To speak of 'conversion' in this case would be absurd. Nevertheless, this does not prevent certain people from writing seriously that Sri Ramakrishna, for example, had 'converted' to Islam during one period of his life and to Christianity during another. Nothing could be more ridiculous than such assertions, which give a rather sorry idea of the authors' mentality. For Sri Ramakrishna it was simply only a kind of 'verification' by direct experience of the validity of the different 'ways' represented by the traditions to which he temporarily assimilated himself. Is there anything in this that could closely or distantly resemble 'conversion' in any way?

Generally speaking, anyone who has an understanding of the unity of traditions, whether through a merely theoretical comprehension or through an effective realization, is necessarily for this very reason 'unconvertible' to anything whatsoever. Moreover, he is the only person who is truly so, since everyone else is always at the mercy of contingent circumstances to some degree. We cannot denounce too vigorously the equivocation that leads certain people to speak of 'conversion' where there is no trace of it, for it is important to put an end to all such nonsense widespread in the profane world, and beneath which it is not difficult to divine intentions that are clearly hostile to everything associated with esoterism.

13

CEREMONIALISM
AND ESTHETICISM

WE HAVE ALREADY DENOUNCED the strange confusion between rites and ceremonies[1] which is often made in our time and which bears testimony to a complete misunderstanding of the true nature and essential characteristics of rites, we might even say of tradition in general. While rites, like everything that is of a truly traditional order, necessarily include a 'non-human' element, ceremonies, on the contrary, are purely human and cannot lay claim to anything more than effects strictly limited to this domain, one could say even to its most outward aspects, for these effects are in reality exclusively 'psychological' and, above all, emotional. Thus one can see in this confusion a particular case or a consequence of 'humanism', that is to say the modern tendency to reduce everything to the human level, a tendency manifested also by the attempt to explain the effects of rites themselves in a 'psychological' way, which effectively abolishes the essential difference between rites and ceremonies.

It is not a question of disputing the relative utility of ceremonies insofar as, by being incidentally joined to rites in a period of spiritual obscuration, they make the latter more accessible to the generality of men, whom they thus prepare as it were to receive the effects of the rites, because they can no longer be immediately reached except by such wholly outward means as the former. Yet in order for this role of 'adjuvant' to remain legitimate and indeed for it to be

1. See *Perspectives on Initiation*, chap. 19.

truly efficacious, the development of ceremonies must be kept within certain limits beyond which they rather risk having completely opposite consequences. This is what one sees only too often in the present state of Western religious forms, where the rites end up being truly smothered by the ceremonies. In such cases not only is the accidental too often taken as the essential, which gives birth to an excessive formalism empty of meaning, but the very 'thickness' of the ceremonial lining, if one may speak thus, presents a far from negligible obstacle to the action of spiritual influences. Here we have a true case of 'solidification' in the sense in which we have taken this word elsewhere,[2] which very much accords with the general character of the modern age.

This abuse, which can be named 'ceremonialism', is something strictly Western, which is easy to understand. Ceremonies always give the impression of something exceptional, and they communicate this appearance to the very rites upon which they have come to be superimposed. Now, the less a civilization is wholly traditional, the more the separation is accentuated between the diminished tradition and everything else, which is now considered purely profane and to constitute what is commonly called 'ordinary life', on which traditional elements no longer exercise any effective influence. It is quite evident that this separation has never been pushed as far as with modern Westerners; and in saying this we naturally mean to speak of those who still have kept something of their tradition but who, outside of the restricted role played in their lives by the 'practice of religion', are in no way distinct from others. In these conditions, everything belonging to tradition must take on the character of an exception with respect to the rest, which precisely emphasizes the display of ceremonies surrounding them. Thus, even granted that this is explained in part by the Western temperament, and that it corresponds to a kind of emotiveness which makes it more particularly sensible to ceremonies, it is nonetheless true that there are also more profound reasons directly linked to the extreme enfeeblement of the traditional spirit. It is also to be noted in this same order of ideas that when Westerners speak of spiritual things, or

2. See *The Reign of Quantity and the Signs of the Times.*

what they rightly or wrongly consider to be such,[3] they feel obliged to take an annoyingly solemn tone, as if better to indicate that these things have nothing in common with the usual subjects of their conversations. Whatever they may think, this affectation of 'ceremoniousness' assuredly has no connection with the dignity and seriousness appropriate to everything of a traditional order, and which never exclude the most perfect naturalness and greatest simplicity of attitude, as one can still see today in the East.[4]

There is another side to the question which we did not mention earlier, but upon which it seems necessary to dwell somewhat. We are speaking of the connection that exists for Westerners between 'ceremonialism' and what can be called 'estheticism'. By this latter word we naturally mean the particular mentality that proceeds from the 'esthetic' point of view, which applies first and most properly to art, but is extended bit by bit to other domains and finally puts a particular 'coloring' on the way that men look at everything. As its name indicates, the 'esthetic' point of view is that which attempts to reduce everything to a simple question of 'sensibility'; this is the modern and profane idea of art which, as A. K. Coomaraswamy has shown in numerous writings, is opposed to its normal and traditional conception. It removes all intellectuality and, one could even say, all intelligibility from whatever it is applied to, and the beautiful, far from being the 'splendor of the true', as it was defined in past

---

3. We add this restriction because of the many counterfeits of spirituality current among our contemporaries; but it suffices that they be convinced that it is spirituality, or that they wish to convince others so, for the same observation to apply in all cases.

4. This is particularly manifest in the case of Islam, which naturally has many rites but not a single ceremony. On the other hand, even in the West one can see in the sermons that have been preserved from the Middle Ages that the preachers of that truly religious period did not at all disdain to use a familiar and sometimes even humorous tone.

A rather significant fact is the deviation current usage has imposed on the word 'pontiff' and its derivatives. For the ordinary Westerner, who is ignorant of their traditional and symbolic value, these words have come to represent nothing more than the most excessive 'ceremonialism', as if the essential function of the pontificate were not the accomplishment of certain rites but only the conducting of particularly pompous ceremonies.

ages, is reduced to no more than whatever produces a certain sentiment of pleasure, and therefore something purely 'psychological' and 'subjective'. It is thus easy to understand how the taste for ceremonies is attached to this point of view, for ceremonies have effects that are only of the esthetic order and could not have any others; just like modern art, they are neither something to be understood nor something with a more or less profound meaning to be penetrated, but are merely leave an 'impression' in a wholly sentimental manner. All of this reaches only the most superficial and illusory part of the psychic being, which varies not only from one individual to another but also within the same individual according to his dispositions of the moment. This sentimental domain is indeed, in all respects, the most complete and the most extreme type of what one could call 'subjectivity' in its pure state.[5]

What we are saying about the taste for ceremonies properly so called also applies of course to the excessive and in a way disproportionate importance that some attribute to everything belonging to outward 'decor', sometimes going so far, even with things of an authentically traditional order, as to make this contingent accessory an indispensable and essential element, while others imagine that rites would lose all their value if not accompanied by more or less 'imposing' ceremonies. It is perhaps even more evident here that this is fundamentally a matter of 'estheticism', and even when those who are thus attached to 'decor' assure us that they are so because of the significance that they recognize in it, we are not certain but that they perhaps deceive themselves and are attracted rather especially by something much more outward and 'subjective', by an 'artistic' impression in the modern sense of the word. The least one can say is that the confusion between the accidental and the essential, which in any case exists, is always the sign of a very imperfect comprehension. Thus, for example, among those who admire the art of the

---

5. We do not have to speak here of certain forms of modern art which can produce the effects of disequilibrium and even 'disintegration', the repercussions of which can be quite far-reaching. This is no longer merely a matter of the insignificance, in the proper sense of the word, that attaches to everything purely profane, but is, indeed, a true work of 'subversion'.

Middle Ages, even when they are sincerely persuaded that their admiration is not simply 'esthetic' as was that of the 'romantics', and that the principal motive is the spirituality expressed by this art, we doubt that there are many who truly understand it and who are capable of making the necessary effort to see it otherwise than with modern eyes, that is, to really place themselves in the state of mind of those who produced this art and of those for whom it was intended. Among those who take pleasure in surrounding themselves with the 'decor' of that period, to a greater or lesser degree one almost always finds, if not strictly speaking the mentality, at least the 'perspective' of the architects who build in 'neo-gothic' style, or of the modern painters who try to imitate the works of 'primitives'. In these reconstitutions there is always something artificial and 'ceremonious', something that 'rings false', one might say, and that rather recalls the 'exhibition' or 'museum' much more than the real and normal use of works of art in a traditional civilization. To say it all in a word, one has the clear impression that the 'spirit' is absent.[6]

What we have just said about the Middle Ages in order to provide an example from the Western world itself could also be said, and with even more reason, in cases of Eastern 'decor'. It is indeed rare that even when composed of authentic elements, these do not rather represent above all the whole idea that Westerners have formed of the East, something having only a very distant relation to what the East really is in itself.[7] This leads us to clarify yet another

6. In the same order of ideas, we will point out incidentally the case of so-called 'folk' festivals so fashionable today. These attempts to reconstitute ancient 'popular' festivals, even when based on the most exact documentation and the most scrupulous erudition, inevitably have a pathetic air of 'masquerade' and of gross counterfeit that could make one believe in an intention to 'parody' that certainly does not exist among their organizers.

7. To take an extreme example, one that is thereby more 'tangible', the works of most of the painters called 'orientalists' show only too well what the Western perspective applied to things of the East can lead to. There is no doubt that they have really taken as their models Oriental people, things and landscapes, but since they have only seen them in a wholly outward fashion, their manner of 'rendering' them is worth about as much as the creations of the 'folklorists' of whom we have just spoken.

important point: among the many manifestations of modern 'estheticism' one must single out the taste for the 'exotic' so frequently witnessed among our contemporaries, a taste which, whatever the different factors that may have contributed to its spread (and which would take too long to examine here in detail), once again finally comes down to a sort of 'artistic' sensibility foreign to any true comprehension, and this, unfortunately, among those who do nothing but 'follow' and imitate others, even to a mere question of fashion, as is the case with the admiration affected for one or another form of art, which varies from one moment to the next according to circumstances. But the case of the 'exotic' concerns us somehow more directly than any other, because it is greatly to be feared that the very interest in Eastern doctrines manifested by some people is too often due to this tendency; when such is the case, it is evident that one is dealing with a purely outward 'attitude' that cannot be taken seriously. What complicates matters is that this same tendency can also be mixed in varying proportions with a much more real and sincere interest; this case is certainly not as hopeless as the other, but what must then be taken into account is that one can never arrive at a true comprehension of any doctrine until the impression of 'exoticism' that it might have had initially should have disappeared entirely. This can require a preliminary effort that is considerable and even painful for some but which is strictly indispensable if they wish to obtain any valid result from the studies they have undertaken. If this is impossible, which naturally sometimes happens, this is because one is dealing with Westerners who, because of their special psychic constitution, can never cease being what they are and who consequently would do much better to remain so entirely and frankly and to renounce occupying themselves with things from which they can draw no real profit, for whatever they do, these things will always be for them in 'another world' having no connection to the one to which they in fact belong and which they are incapable to leaving. We will add that these remarks are particularly important in the case of Westerners by birth who, for one reason or another, and especially for reasons of an esoteric and initiatic order—the only reasons we can consider worthy of interest[8]—have decided to join an Eastern tradition; in fact, here we have a true question of 'qualification' which is imposed on them and which in all strictness ought to be the object of a sort of preliminary 'trial' before any question of a real and effective adherence. In any case, and even in the most favorable conditions, such people must be very much convinced that, as long as they find the slightest 'exotic' character in the traditional form they have adopted, this is incontestable proof that they have not truly assimilated the form, and that, whatever the appearances, it remains something exterior to their real being and modifies it only superficially. This is one of the first obstacles such people encounter on their way, and experience obliges us to recognize that, for many, this is perhaps not the least difficult to overcome.

8. On this subject, see the preceding chapter, 'Conversions'.

14

RECENT
CONFUSIONS

A FEW YEARS AGO we had to report the strange attitude of those who feel the need to deliberately confuse esoterism with mysticism, or even, speaking more exactly, to expound things in such a way as to entirely substitute mysticism for esoterism whenever they encounter it, particularly in Eastern doctrines.[1] This confusion first arose among the orientalists, and at the beginning may have simply been due to their incomprehension, of which there are so many other proofs that one need not be too surprised at it. But the matter becomes much more serious when in certain religious circles this confusion is seized upon for motives that are visibly much more conscious and with a prejudice that is no longer merely one of forcing everything willy-nilly into Western categories. These circles were formerly content simply with denying the existence of all esoterism, which is obviously the easiest attitude because it dispenses with the need to examine more deeply something that is particularly inconvenient, which it is for those who, like the exclusive exoterists, claim that nothing escapes their competence. But it seems that at a certain moment they realized that this total and 'simplistic' negation was no longer possible and that it was also more clever to misrepresent esoterism in such a way as to 'annex' it by assimilating it to something which, like mysticism, really belongs only to religious exoterism. Thus one could still forego use of the word esoterism, since the word mysticism everywhere took its place, and the

1. See *Perspectives on Initiation*, chap. 1.

thing itself was thereby so travestied that it seemed to enter into the exoteric domain, which was no doubt what was essential for their proposed aims and allowed some people to make random 'judgments' about things they were not in the least qualified to appreciate and which, by their true nature, were from every point of view entirely outside their 'jurisdiction'.

Most recently we have noted yet another change of attitude, and, we will freely say, a change of tactics, for it goes without saying that in all of this it is not simply a matter of an attitude which, as erroneous as it may be, could at least pass for being disinterested, as one can concede in the case of most orientalists.[2] What is rather curious is that this new attitude began to show itself precisely in the same circles as the preceding, as well as in others which adhered rather closely to them, judging from the fact that the same people appear in both.[3] Now, there is no longer any hesitation to speak plainly of esoterism, as if this word had suddenly ceased to be frightening to certain people; what could have happened to make them come to this point? No doubt it would be rather difficult to say exactly, but one is permitted to suppose that in one way or another the existence of esoterism has become too evident a truth for them to continue to pass over in silence, or to hold that esoterism is nothing more than mysticism; to tell the truth, we fear that we ourselves count for something in the rather painful discomfiture that this finding must have caused in these circles, but that is the way things are and we can do nothing about it. One must resign oneself to it and do one's best to accommodate oneself to changes in the circumstances of the milieu in which one lives! This moreover is what people are keen to

2. We say 'most' for obviously an exception must be made for certain orientalists who are found to have at the same time more or less close links with the religious circles in question.

3. We have already given an example of the attitude in question in our recent book reviews, in connection with a new book, and we will shortly have occasion to give others. But it is well understood that for the moment we are keeping to more general considerations, without going into the particular and detailed examination of certain individual cases (and we also mean groups and their agents as well as individual persons), which will be better done elsewhere at the appropriate place.

do, but this is not to say that we must congratulate ourselves over-much, for there are hardly any illusions about what one could call the 'quality' of this change. Indeed, it is not sufficient for us that the existence of esoterism as such finally be recognized; it is also neces-sary for us to see how it is presented and how it is discussed, and, as we ought to have expected, it is just here that things deteriorate in a rather singular way.

First of all, these people seem to admit not only the existence of esoterism but also, to a degree, its validity, especially under the cover of symbolism, although it is not always easy to know what some of them really think because they seem to try hard never to dispel entirely the ambiguities that enter into their writings (and we do not wish to wrong them by believing that this is solely incompe-tence on their part); and surely it is already something appreciable that, as regards symbolism, they are no longer content with the annoying banality of current exoteric interpretations and the shal-low 'moralism' which usually inspires them. Nonetheless, we will readily say that in certain respects, they sometimes go too far in the sense that, to these very legitimate considerations, they mix others from a wholly fantastic pseudo-symbolism that is impossible to take seriously. Should one see here only the effect of a certain inexperi-ence in this domain where nothing can be improvised? Something of this is very possible, but there may also be something else; one could even say that this mélange is expressly made to devalue sym-bolism and esoterism, and yet we cannot believe that this is the intention of those who write these things, for they would then have to resign themselves to seeing this discredit recoil upon themselves and their own work. But it is less certain that this intention does not exist in any way among those who direct them, for it goes without saying that in such cases all are not equally conscious of the under-lying motives for the 'tactics' in which they collaborate. However this may be, until we have proof to the contrary we prefer to think that what is involved is only a 'minimizing' of the esoterism they can no longer deny (this is what a proverb calls 'keeping the fire from spreading'), of reducing its scope as much as possible by intro-ducing questions that are of no real importance, and that are even wholly insignificant, 'amusements' for a public that is naturally only too disposed to form an idea of esoterism itself after these little things which, much more than all the rest, are to the measure of its powers of comprehension.[4]

This however is not what is most serious; there is something else that seems even more disquieting in certain respects: the inextricable mixing of true esoterism with its many contemporary deformations and counterfeits, occultist, Theosophist, and others, and the practice of drawing notions and references from each indiscriminately and then presenting them as if they were all on the same plane so to speak, while refraining from indicating clearly what one accepts and what one rejects. Is this only ignorance or a lack of discernment? Indeed, these latter may often play a role in such cases, and moreover the 'directors' often know very well how to use them for their own ends; but it is unfortunately impossible for this to be all there is to the present case, for we are entirely certain that among those who act thus are those who are perfectly aware of what is really happening. How then should we qualify this way of proceeding, which seems expressly calculated to cause trouble and confusion in the minds of their readers? Besides, since this is not an isolated case but a general tendency among those of whom we speak, it indeed seems that a 'preconceived' plan is involved; naturally one can see in this a new example of the modern disorder that more and more extends everywhere, and without which confusions of this kind could scarcely occur, much less spread. But this is not a sufficient explanation and once again we must ask what more precise intentions underlie all of this? Perhaps it is too early to distinguish them clearly, and it is best to wait a while in order to see in what direction this 'movement' will develop; but when everything is

---

4. We know of one ecclesiastic who, after expounding views of incontestable interest about symbolism, later thought himself obliged, not to renounce them, but to attenuate them by declaring that he attached to them only a very secondary importance and considered them doctrinally insignificant. This seems to support what we were saying about the deliberate 'belittling' of esoterism, which moreover can be accomplished in many apparently contrary ways by making out as important what is not so, and by belittling what really is.

thus confounded, is it not in the first place a question of transferring to authentic esoterism something of the suspicion that very legitimately attaches to its counterfeits? This might seem to contradict the very acceptance of esoterism, but we are not quite sure that this is really so, and this is why. First, the very fact of the ambiguities to which we alluded above means that this acceptance is only 'in principle' as it were and does not actually bears on anything clearly defined; then, although they refrain from any assessment of the whole, from time to time they throw out malicious insinuations, which almost always happen to be directed against true esoterism. These remarks lead one to ask whether in the final analysis it is simply a matter of preparing the establishment of a new pseudo-esoterism of a rather particular kind meant to give an appearance of satisfaction to those who are no longer content with exoterism, while at the same time diverting them from the true esoterism to which they intend to oppose it.[5] If this is the case, since this pseudo-esoterism—of which perhaps we already have a few samples in the fantasies and the 'amusements' mentioned—is probably still quite far from being entirely 'complete', it would be understandable that, while waiting for it to be so, they should have every interest in remaining vague, with the idea of going forth and openly taking the offensive at the right moment, and in this way all would be quite well explained. Of course, until we know more we can only present what we have just said as a hypothesis, but all who know the mentality of certain people will surely recognize that it does not lack plausibility; and as for ourselves, for some time now we have received from various sources accounts of claimed initiations that, however inconsistent they may be, also confirm this.

We do not wish to say anything more about this for the moment, but we were obliged not to wait longer to warn those who, with the best faith in the world, risk letting themselves be too easily seduced

---

5. The incorporation of certain really traditional elements does not prevent it, as a 'construction' and as a whole, from being only a pseudo-esoterism; besides, the occultists themselves have proceeded in this way, although for different reasons and much less consciously.

by certain deceptive appearances; and we will be only too happy if, as sometimes happens, the mere fact of exposing these things is sufficient to arrest their development before they go too far. We will add that, at a much lower level than this, we have recently also observed confusions which are in the final analysis of the same sort, and with these at least the intention is in no way doubtful: this is manifestly to try to assimilate esoterism with its worst counterfeits, and the representatives of traditional initiatic organizations with the charlatans of the various pseudo-initiations. There is assuredly a difference between these crude ignominies, against which one cannot protest too strongly, and certain much more subtle maneuvers; but fundamentally does not all of this tend in the same direction, and are not the most clever and insidious attempts, by this very fact, also the most dangerous?

15

'INTELLECTUAL PRIDE'

IN THE FOREGOING CHAPTER about the new attitude taken toward esoterism in certain religious circles we said that from time to time, and as it were incidentally, the accounts concerning this order of things introduce certain ill-willed insinuations which, even if not a result of any well-defined intention, nevertheless accord poorly with the very admission of esoterism, be this admission only as it were 'in principle'. Among these insinuations is one we think it not pointless to reexamine more particularly. This is the reproach of 'intellectual pride', which is certainly nothing new—far from it—but which reappears here once again and, rather strangely, is always aimed at those who adhere to the most authentically traditional esoteric doctrines. Must one thereby conclude that they are considered to be more troublesome than the counterfeiters of all kinds? This is indeed very possible, and in such cases moreover the counterfeiters are doubtless rather to be regarded as having to be treated gently since, as we have noted, they create the most troubling confusions and by this very fact are auxiliaries (assuredly involuntary but no less useful for all that) of the new 'tactic' believed to be necessary in confronting the circumstances.

The expression 'intellectual pride' is manifestly self-contradictory, for if words still have a definite meaning—but we are sometimes tempted to doubt this is so for most of our contemporaries—pride can only be of a purely sentimental order. In a certain sense one could speak of pride in connection with reason because this belongs to the individual order just as sentiment does, so that between the one and the other reciprocal reactions are always possible. But how could this be so in the order of pure intellectuality, which is essentially supra-individual? And once it is by hypothesis a matter of esoterism, it is obvious that there can be no question of reason but only of the transcendent intellect, either directly, as in the case of true metaphysical and initiatic realization, or at least indirectly, but yet also quite real, as in the case of knowledge that is still merely theoretical, since in each case it is a question of things that reason is incapable of attaining. This moreover is why the rationalists are always so bent on denying its existence; esoterism inconveniences them as much as it does the most exclusive religious exo-terists, although naturally for very different reasons; but, motives aside, this is in fact a rather curious 'conjunction'.

At bottom, the reproach in question might seem to be inspired above all by the modern mania for equality that will not suffer anything that surpasses the 'average'; but what is most astonishing is to see similar prejudices, which are the sign of a clearly anti-traditional mentality shared by people who claim a tradition, even if only from the exoteric point of view. This certainly proves that they are seriously affected by the modern spirit, although they probably are not aware of it themselves; and this is yet one more of the contradictions so frequent in our time which one is really obliged to note even while one is astonished that they should generally pass so unnoticed. But this contradiction reaches its most extreme degree when it is found, not among those who are resolved to admit nothing other than exoterism and declare this expressly, but, as here, among those who seem to accept a certain esoterism, whatever be its value and authenticity, for after all they should at least realize that the same reproach could also be made against them by intransigent exoterists. Must it be concluded from this that their claim to esoterism ultimately is only a mask, and that its purpose is above all to bring back to the 'herd' those who might be tempted to leave it were a way not found to divert them from true esoterism? If this were so, it would explain everything quite nicely, with the accusation of 'intellectual pride' then raised up before them as a sort of bogeyman, while at the same time the presentation of some pseudo-esoterism or other would give their aspirations an illusory and wholly inoffensive satisfaction. Once again, to deny the plausibility of this hypothesis would presume of very defective knowledge of the mentality of certain circles.

Now, regarding this alleged 'intellectual pride', we can go further toward the heart of the matter. It would be a strange pride indeed that ends by denying any value to the individuality in itself by making it appear as strictly null in comparison with the Principle. In short, this reproach proceeds from exactly the same incomprehension as that of egoism, which is sometimes also leveled at anyone who seeks to attain final Deliverance. How can one speak of 'egoism' where by very definition there is no longer any ego? It would be, if not more just, at least more logical, to see egoism in the preoccupation with 'salvation' (which does not, of course, at all mean that the latter is illegitimate), or to find the mark of a certain pride in the desire to 'immortalize' the individuality instead of striving to go beyond it. The exoterists ought well to reflect on this, for it would make them a bit more circumspect in the accusations they hurl so thoughtlessly. In connection with the being that attains Deliverance, we will further add that such realization of a universal order has consequences that are very much more extensive and effective than common 'altruism', which is but a concern for the interests of a mere collectivity and which consequently in no way leaves the individual order; in the supra-individual order where there is no longer any 'I', there is likewise no longer any 'other', because this is a domain where all beings are one, 'fused but not confused' according to Eckhart's expression, and thereby they truly realize the words of Christ, 'That they may be one even as the Father and I are one.'

What is true of pride is equally true of humility, which, being its contrary, is situated exactly on the same level, and which has the same exclusively sentimental and individual character. But, in a wholly different order, there is something which, spiritually, is much more valuable than this humility, and this is 'spiritual poverty' understood in its true meaning, that is the recognition one's total dependence on the Principle; and who could have a more real and more complete consciousness of this than true esoterists? We will go even further: today, who other than these is still truly aware of this to any degree; and even among the adherents of traditional exoterism, except perhaps for certain ever rarer exceptions, is there anything more than a wholly verbal and outward affirmation of this? We strongly doubt it for this profound reason: to use the terms of the Far-Eastern tradition, which allow us to express most easily what we want to say here, the fully 'normal' man must be *yin* with respect to the Principle, but to the Principle alone, and by reason of his 'central' position he must be *yang* in relation to all manifestation. On the contrary, fallen man adopts an attitude by which he tends more and more to become *yang* in relation to the Principle (or rather gives himself the illusion of doing so, for it goes without saying that this is an impossibility) and *yin* in relation to manifestation; and it is from this that both pride and humility are born. When the fall reaches its last phase, pride finally results in the negation of the Principle, and humility the negation of all hierarchy; the religious exoterists obviously refuse the first of these two negations; indeed, they reject it with a true horror when it takes on the name of atheism. But, on the contrary, we often have the impression that they are not very far removed from the second![1]

---

1. We will take advantage of this occasion to note in passing a particularly grotesque reproach made against us which, in the final analysis, belongs to the same order of ideas, that is to say the intrusion of sentimentality into a domain to which it has no legitimate access. It seems that our writings have the serious defect of 'lacking joy'! That certain things bring us joy or not depends in any case only on our own individual dispositions, and in themselves these things have nothing to do with the matter, being wholly independent of such contingencies. This cannot and must not be of interest to anyone, and it would be perfectly ridiculous and improper to introduce anything like this into an exposition of traditional doctrines in regard to which individualities, ours as well as any other's, count for absolutely nothing.

16

DIRECT CONTEMPLATION AND REFLECTED CONTEMPLATION

ONCE AGAIN we must return to the essential differences between metaphysical or initiatic realization and mystical realization, for certain people have asked the following question on this subject: if, as we shall explain later, contemplation is the highest form of activity, much more active in reality than anything arising from outward action, and if, as is generally admitted, there is also contemplation in the case of mystical states, is this something incompatible with the character of passivity inherent in mysticism? Moreover, once one speaks of contemplation both in the metaphysical and in the mystical order, it might seem that the two coincide in this respect, at least in a certain measure; or, if this is not so, are there then two kinds of contemplation?

Before all else it is appropriate to recall in this regard that there are many different degrees of mysticism and that the lower forms are not in question here, for with these one cannot really speak of contemplation in the true sense of the word. From this point of view we must set aside all that has a clearly 'phenomenal' character, that is to say, in sum, all those states where one encounters what the theoreticians of mysticism designate as 'sensible visions' and 'imaginary visions' (although the imagination belongs equally among the sensible faculties taken in the widest sense), states which they themselves consider to be inferior and which indeed they consider only with a certain mistrust, and with good reason, for it is evident that it is here that illusion can most easily be introduced. There is no mystical contemplation properly speaking except in the case of what is called 'intellectual vision', which is of a much more 'interior' order and which only what might be called the higher mystics attain, to the point that it seems that this is in a way the result and the very goal of their realization; but do these mystics thereby effectively transcend the individual domain? This is what the question comes down to, for leaving aside the differences in methods that respectively characterize the initiatic and mystical paths, it is this alone that might justify as regards their goal a certain assimilation like that just mentioned. Of course there is no question of diminishing the extent of the qualitative differences within mysticism itself; but it is no less true that, even for what is highest in mysticism, this assimilation implies a confusion that must be dispelled.

Clearly, there are really two kinds of contemplation, which could be called direct contemplation and reflected contemplation. Just as the sun can be looked at directly or only in its reflection in the water, so spiritual realities can likewise be contemplated as they are in themselves or in their reflection in the individual domain. In both cases, one can indeed speak of contemplation, and in a certain sense it is even the same realities that are contemplated, just as it is the same sun that is seen directly or in its reflection; but it is no less evident that there is a very great difference between them. There is an even greater difference than one might at first think from the comparison just given, for the direct contemplation of spiritual realities necessarily implies that one rise to their own domain as it were, which presupposes a certain degree of realization of supraindividual states, a realization that can never be anything but essentially active. On the contrary, reflected contemplation implies only that one 'open oneself' to what 'spontaneously' presents itself (and which may also not present itself, for this is something that in no way depends on the will or initiative of the contemplative), and this is why there is nothing here that is incompatible with mystical passivity. Naturally, this does not prevent contemplation from always being, at one degree or another, a true interior activity; and besides, a state that is purely passive cannot even be conceived, for in a certain respect even mere sensation has something active about it; in fact, pure passivity belongs only to *materia prima* and can never be found anywhere in manifestation. But the passivity of the mystic consists properly in the fact that he is limited to receiving what comes to him, and this indeed cannot fail to awaken in him a certain interior activity, which precisely constitutes his contemplation; but he is passive because he does nothing to go toward the realities that are the object of this contemplation, and this entails as consequence that he does not leave his individual state. In order that these realities become accessible to him, it is thus necessary that they descend so to speak into the individual domain or, if one prefers, that they be reflected there, as we have just said. This last way of speaking is moreover the most exact because it allows one better to understand that these spiritual realities are in no way affected by their apparent 'descent', any more than is the sun by the existence of its reflection.

Another particularly important point, which is very closely related to the preceding, is that mystical contemplation, by the very fact that it is indirect, never implies an identification but on the contrary always leaves the duality between subject and object. To tell the truth, it is in a way necessary that it be thus, for this duality forms an integral part of the religious point of view as such and, as we have often had the occasion to say, all mysticism properly belongs to the religious domain.[1] What can lead to confusion on this point is that the mystics readily use the word 'union', and that the contemplation in question belongs even more precisely to what they call the 'unitive life'; but this 'union' does not at all have the same meaning as *Yoga* or its equivalents, so that there is only a wholly outward similarity. It is not illegitimate to use the same word, for even in current language one speaks of union between beings in many different cases where there is obviously no degree of

---

1. This is not to say that in ancient Christian writings there are not certain things that cannot be understood otherwise than as the more or less explicit affirmation of an identification; but the moderns, who in any case generally try to minimize the meaning of these texts since they find it inconvenient that they do not fit into their own conceptions, err in relating them to mysticism. At that time, even in Christianity, there were certainly many things of a wholly different order, of which they have not the faintest idea.

identification between them, but it is always necessary to take the greatest care not to confuse different things under the pretext that a single word is used to designate them both. Let us again emphasize that in mysticism there is never any question of identification with the Principle, nor even with one of its 'non-supreme' aspects (which in any case would manifestly transcend possibilities of an individual order); and further, the union that is considered as the very end of the mystical life is always related to a principal manifestation envisaged solely in the human domain or in relation to it.[2]

It must be clearly understood, on the other hand, that the contemplation attained in initiatic realization includes many different degrees, so that it assuredly does not always go as far as identification; but in such cases it is regarded only as a preliminary step, a stage in the course of realization, and never as the highest goal to which initiation ought finally lead.[3] This should suffice to show that the two paths do not really lead to the same end, for one of them stops at what for the other is but a secondary stage; furthermore, even at this degree there is the great difference that in one of the two cases it is a reflection that is contemplated in itself and for itself, as it were, while in the other this reflection is taken only as the end-point of rays that must be followed in order to re-ascend from there to the very source of the light.

2. The very language of the mystics is very clear in this regard: it is never a question of union with the Christ Principle, that is with the *Logos* in itself, which, even without going so far as identification, would already be above the human domain; it is always 'union with Christ Jesus', an expression that clearly refers in an exclusive way only to the 'individualized' aspect of the *Avatāra*.

3. The difference between this preliminary contemplation and identification is that which exists between what the Islamic tradition respectively designates as *'ayn al-yaqīn* and *ḥaqq al-yaqīn* (see *Perspectives on Initiation*, chap. 24, n9).

17

DOCTRINE
AND METHOD

WE HAVE OFTEN EMPHASIZED the fact that, if the ultimate goal of all initiation is essentially one, it is nonetheless necessary that the paths enabling it to be reached be many in order to conform to the diversity of individual conditions; for one must not consider only the point of arrival, which is always the same, but also the point of departure, which differs according to the individual. Moreover, it goes without saying that these many ways become more unified in the measure that they approach the goal, and that even before this is reached there is a point after which individual differences can no longer intervene in any way; and it is no less evident that their multiplicity, which in no way affects the unity of the goal, could no longer affect the fundamental unity of the doctrine which is really nothing other than that of truth itself.

These notions are entirely current in all Eastern civilizations; thus in Arab countries it has become a proverbial expression to say that 'each shaykh has his *ṭarīqah*', meaning that there are many ways to do the same thing and to obtain the same result. To the multiplicity of *ṭuruq* in Islamic initiation exactly correspond the paths of *Yoga* in the Hindu tradition, which are sometimes spoken of as so many distinct *Yogas* although this use of the plural is completely improper if the word be taken in its strict sense, which designates the goal itself. It is only justified by the usual extension of the same denomination to the methods or procedures that are used to attain this goal; and in all rigor it would be more correct to say that there is only one *Yoga* but many *mārgas* or paths leading to its realization.

Among certain Westerners we have noted a truly strange misunderstanding in this regard: from the multiplicity of paths they try to conclude the non-existence of a single and invariable doctrine, or even of any doctrine at all, in *Yoga*; they thus confuse, as unlikely as this might seem, the question of doctrine and the question of method, which are things belonging to entirely different orders. Moreover, if one adheres to exactness of expression, one should not speak of 'a doctrine of *Yoga*' but of traditional Hindu doctrine, of which *Yoga* represents an aspect; and as for methods of realizing *Yoga*, these belong only to the 'technical' applications which arise from a doctrine and are themselves also traditional precisely because they are established on the basis of the doctrine and are ordered in conformity to it, their aim being, in the final analysis, the achieving of pure Knowledge. It is very clear that a doctrine, to be truly what it should be, must include in its very unity different aspects or points of view (*darshanas*), and that within each of these points of view it must be susceptible of indefinitely varied applications. To imagine that this is something contrary to its unity and its essential invariability one must, let us say it clearly, lack the least idea of what a traditional doctrine really is. Moreover, in an analogous way, is not the indefinite multiplicity of contingent things also contained entirely in the unity of their Principle, and this without the immutability of the Principle being in any way affected?

It is not enough simply to point out an error or misunderstanding such as the one involved here; it is more instructive to seek out an explanation for it, and so we must ask what in the Western mentality could correspond to the negation of the existence of something like traditional Hindu doctrine. Indeed, it is better to take this error in its most general and most extreme form, for it is only thus that it is possible to discover its very root; the more particular and attenuated forms that it sometimes takes on will then be explained *a fortiori*, and besides, they really do hardly anything more than conceal the radical 'negation' we have just described, although no doubt unconsciously in many cases. Indeed, to deny the unity and invariability of a doctrine is in the final analysis to deny its most essential and most fundamental characteristics, those without which it no longer merits the name; it is in truth to deny the very existence of the doctrine as such, even if those who do so do not realize it.

First of all, insofar as it claims to be based on the diversity of methods, as we have just said, this negation obviously proceeds from an incapacity to go beyond outer appearances and perceive the unity underneath their multiplicity; in this respect it is of the same kind as the negation of the fundamental and principial unity of all traditions because of the existence of different traditional forms, which in reality are nothing but so many expressions in which the one and only tradition clothes itself in order to adapt itself to different conditions of time and place, just as the different methods of realization in each traditional form are only so many means it employs to make itself accessible to the diversity of individuals. However, this is only the most superficial aspect of the question. In order to go to the heart of things it must be said that this same negation also shows that, when speaking of doctrine as we are doing here, certain people completely misunderstand what is really involved. Indeed, if they did not divert the word from its normal meaning they could not dispute that it applies to a case like that of the Hindu tradition and that it is even only in such a case, that is, in the case of a traditional doctrine, that it possesses all the fullness of its meaning. Now, if this misunderstanding exists, it is because most present-day Westerners cannot conceive of a doctrine otherwise than under either of two particular forms, of very unequal quality moreover, since one is exclusively profane while the other has a truly traditional character, though both are specifically Western. These two forms are the philosophical system and religious dogma.

Having said often enough that traditional truth can never be expressed in a systematic form, we need not dwell on it again. Furthermore, the apparent unity of a system, which results merely from its more or less narrow limitations, is strictly only a parody of true doctrinal unity. In addition, every philosophy is no more than an individual construction which, as such, attaches to no transcendent principle and consequently lacks any authority. It is therefore not a doctrine in the true sense of the word, and we would say that it is rather a pseudo-doctrine, understanding by this that, although it claims to be one, its claim is wholly unjustified. Naturally, modern

Westerners think quite differently about this, and they are truly at a loss where they find none of their accustomed pseudo-doctrinal frameworks; but since they will not or cannot admit this, they distort it by striving all the same to force everything into these frameworks, or, if they cannot succeed at this, they simply declare that what is involved is not doctrine, by one of those reversals of the normal order to which they are accustomed. Besides, since they confuse the intellectual with the rational, they also confuse doctrine with mere 'speculation', and, since traditional doctrine is something completely different from the former, they cannot understand what it is. Philosophy will certainly not inform them that theoretical knowledge, being indirect and imperfect, has in itself only a 'preparatory' value, in the sense of furnishing instruction on how not to go astray in pursuit of realization, realization being the only way to obtain effective knowledge, the existence and very possibility of which they do not even suspect. Thus, when we say as we did above that the goal to be attained is pure Knowledge, how could they know what we mean?

On the other hand, we have taken great care to specify throughout our works that the orthodoxy of traditional Hindu doctrine must never be conceived in a religious mode. This necessarily implies that it can never be expressed in dogmatic form, which is inapplicable outside the strictly religious point of view. But in fact, Westerners do not generally know any other form of traditional truths except this one, which is why they inevitably think of dogmatic formulas when the subject of doctrinal orthodoxy is raised. They know at least what a dogma is, which is certainly not to say that they understand what it means; but they know the outer appearance under which it presents itself and every idea they still have of tradition is limited to this. The anti-traditional spirit, which is that of the modern West, enters into a fury at the mere idea of dogma, because, in its ignorance of all the other forms it can take, this is how tradition appears to them. The West would never have come to its present state of decay and confusion had it remained faithful to its dogmas, for to adapt to its particular mental conditions tradition was obliged to take on this special aspect, at least in its exoteric part. This last restriction is indispensable, for it must be well understood that in the esoteric and initiatic order there never could have been any question of dogma, even in the West; but these are things the very memory of which is too completely lost by modern Westerners to provide terms of comparison that might help them understand what other traditional forms might be. On the other hand, if dogma does not exist everywhere, this is because even in the exoteric order it would not have the same raison d'être as in the West. There are people who in order not to 'divagate', in the etymological sense of the word, need to be kept under strict supervision, while there are others who have no such need; dogma is necessary for the first and not for the second, just as, to take another example of a slightly different kind, the forbidding of images is necessary only for people who naturally tend toward a kind of anthropomorphism; and doubtless one could easily show that dogma is bound up with the special traditional organizational form represented by the constitution of a 'church', which is also something specifically Western.

This is not the place to dwell longer on these last points, but we can say the following in conclusion. When it is complete, traditional doctrine by its very essence has truly unlimited possibilities; it is therefore vast enough to include within its orthodoxy all aspects of the truth, but it can never include anything other than this, and this is precisely what is signified by the word orthodoxy, which excludes only error, but excludes it absolutely. Easterners, and more generally all peoples with a traditional civilization, have always ignored what modern Westerners dignify with the name of 'tolerance', which is really nothing but indifference to truth, that is to say something that can only be conceived where intellectuality is wholly absent. Is not the fact that Westerners vaunt this 'tolerance' as a virtue a very striking measure of the debasement to which the denial of tradition has led them?

18

THE THREE WAYS
AND THE
INITIATIC FORMS

IT IS KNOWN that the Hindu tradition distinguishes three 'paths' (*mārgas*), which are, respectively, those of *Karma, Bhakti,* and *Jñāna*. We shall not go into the definition of these terms, which we suppose are sufficiently known to our readers; but before all else we shall specify that, since these terms correspond to three forms of *Yoga*, this essentially implies that all have or are susceptible of having a properly initiatic meaning.[1] Furthermore, it must be clearly understood that every distinction of this kind inevitably has always a certain 'schematic' and somewhat theoretical character, for spiritual 'paths' in fact vary indefinitely to suit the diversity of individual natures; and even in a very general classification like this it can only be a question of a predominance of one element over the others, without the others ever being entirely excluded. This case is like that of the *gunas*: beings are classified according to the *guna* that predominates in them, but it goes without saying that the nature of every manifested being nonetheless includes all the *gunas* at once, although in different proportions, for it is impossible that it should be otherwise with everything that proceeds from *Prakriti*. Besides, the connection that we are making between these two cases is more

---

1. We say 'are susceptible of having' because they also can have an exoteric meaning, but it is obvious that this is not involved when it is a question of *Yoga*. Naturally, the initiatic meaning is like a transposition of the exoteric meaning into a higher order.

than a mere comparison, and is all the more justified in that there really is a certain correlation between the two. *Jñāna-mārga* is obviously the path appropriate to *sattvic* beings, while *Bhakti-mārga* and *Karma-mārga* suit those whose nature is chiefly 'rajasic', but with different nuances; in a certain sense one could say that in the last there is something closer to *tamas* than there is in the previous path, but we must not push this consideration too far, for it is quite clear that beings of 'tamasic' nature are in no way qualified to follow any initiatic path at all.

Whatever the case with this last reservation, it is no less true that a connection exists between the respective characters of the three *mārgas* and the constitutive elements of the being divided according to the ternary 'spirit, soul, body'.[2] In itself, pure Knowledge is of an essentially supra-individual order, that is to say in the final analysis spiritual, like the transcendent intellect to which it belongs; the clearly psychic character of *Bhakti* is evident, while *Karma* in all its modalities necessarily includes a certain activity of a corporeal order and, whatever the transpositions of which these terms are susceptible, something of this original nature must inevitably be found there. This fully confirms what we said concerning the correspondence with the *gunas*. The *jñānic* path, in these conditions, is obviously suited only to beings in whom the ascending tendency of *sattva* predominates and who, by this very fact, are predisposed to aim directly at the realization of higher states instead of waiting for a detailed development of individual possibilities; the two other paths, on the contrary, begin by appealing to properly individual elements, if only to transform them finally into something belonging to a higher order, and this indeed conforms to the nature of *rajas*, which is the tendency producing the expansion of the being on the level of individuality, which, it must not be forgotten, is composed of the totality of psychic and bodily elements. An immediate consequence of this is that the *jñānic* path refers more particularly to the 'greater mysteries' and the *bhaktic* and *karmic* paths to the

2. Here again one must not see anything exclusive in such a correspondence, for every initiatic path necessarily implies a participation of the whole being if it is to be truly valid.

'lesser mysteries'; in other words, this shows once again that it is only by *Jñāna* that one can attain the final goal, while *Bhakti* and *Karma* have rather a 'preparatory' role, for the corresponding paths lead only to a certain point but make possible the attainment of Knowledge for those whose nature would not have the aptitude for it directly and without such a preparation. Moreover, it should be understood that even for the primary stages there could of course be no effective initiation without a degree of real knowledge, even when, in the methods used, the 'accent' is put above all on the *bhaktic* or *karmic* element. But what we wish to emphasize is that in any case, beyond the limits of the individual state, there can be only a single and unique path which is necessarily that of pure Knowledge. Another consequence that we must also note is that, because of the connection of the *bhaktic* and *karmic* paths with the domain of individual possibilities and with the 'lesser mysteries', the distinction between the two is much less clear-cut than that with the *jñanic* path, something which must naturally be reflected in the relationships between the corresponding initiatic forms; we shall have to return to this point later in our account.

These considerations lead us to consider yet another relationship, that existing generally between the three *mārgas* and the three 'twice-born' castes. It is moreover easy to understand why there must be such a relationship, since the distinction of castes is nothing else in principle than a classification of human beings according to their individual natures, and it is precisely in conformity with the diversity of these natures that there exists a plurality of paths. The Brahmins, being of a *sattvic* nature, are particularly qualified for *Jñāna-mārga*, and it is expressly said that they must strive as directly as possible toward a possession of the higher states of being; moreover, their very function in traditional society is essentially and before all else a function of knowledge. The two other castes, whose nature is principally *rajasic*, exercise functions that in themselves do not transcend the individual level and are oriented toward outward activity;[3] those of the Kshatriyas correspond to what one might call

---

3. We say 'in themselves' because they can be transformed by an initiation that takes them as a support.

the 'psyche' of the collectivity and those of the Vaishyas have as their object the different necessities of the corporeal order. From this, given what we said earlier, it results that the Kshatriyas are especially qualified for *Bhakti-mārga* and the Vaishyas for *Karma-mārga*, and in fact it is just this that can be discerned generally in the initiatic forms respectively intended for them. However there is an important remark to be made in this connection: if *Karma-mārga* is understood in its widest sense, it is defined by *svadharma*, that is, by each being's accomplishment of the function that conforms to its proper nature; one could then envisage this as applied to all the castes, although the term would be manifestly inappropriate with regard to the Brahmins, whose function is really beyond the domain of action. But it can at least be applied to both Kshatriyas and Vaishyas, although with different modalities, and this is an example of the difficulty, as we said earlier, of separating in an entirely clear way what is appropriate to the one or the other; and it is known that the *Bhagavad Gītā* describes a *Karma-Yoga* that is particularly intended for Kshatriyas. Despite this, it still remains true that, if the words are taken in their strictest sense, the initiations of the Kshatriyas present in their totality a particularly 'bhaktic' character, while those of the Vaishyas have a chiefly 'karmic' one; and this will shortly become clearer by an example taken from the initiatic forms of the Western world itself.

Indeed, it goes without saying that when we speak of the castes as we do here, referring primarily to the Hindu tradition for the convenience of our explanation and because it furnishes us with the most adequate terminology in this regard, what we say of them applies equally to everything that elsewhere corresponds in one form or another to these castes, for the main categories among which the individual natures of human beings are divided are always and everywhere the same, for the very reason that reduced to their principle they are nothing but a result of the respective predominance of the different *gunas*, which obviously applies to all of humanity inasmuch as it is a particular case of a law that is valid for the totality of universal manifestation. The only notable difference is in the greater or lesser proportion, according to conditions of time and place, of men who belong to each of these categories, and who, if they are qualified to receive initiation, are consequently capable of following one or the other of the corresponding paths;[4] in the most extreme case it can happen that one of these paths might practically cease to exist in a given milieu when the number of those suited to follow it becomes insufficient to maintain a distinct initiatic form.[5] This is what happened notably in the West where, at least for a very long while, the aptitudes for knowledge have steadily become much rarer and less developed than the tendency toward action, which amounts to saying that in the entirety of the Western world, even among those who form the 'elite', if only a relative one, *rajas* greatly outweighs *sattva*. In addition, even as early as the Middle Ages one does not find clear indications of the existence of strictly *jñānic* initiatic forms which normally should have corresponded to sacerdotal initiation, this to the point that even the initiatic organizations which were most particularly linked to certain religious orders had a very strongly accentuated *bhaktic* character, as far as one can judge from the manner of expression most often used by those members who left written records. On the other hand, at this period one finds both chivalric initiation, the dominant character of which is obviously *bhaktic*,[6] and the craft initiations, which were *karmic* in the strictest sense, since they were essentially based on the effective exercise of a craft. It goes without saying that the first was a Kshatriya initiation and that the second were Vaishya initiations, taking the caste designations in the general sense just now explained; additionally, the links that have almost always existed in fact between these two categories, as we have often

4. In order not to complicate our account unnecessarily, we shall not introduce here the question of anomalies which, today, especially in the West, result from the 'mingling of castes', from the ever growing difficulty of determining exactly each man's true nature, and from the fact that most people no longer fill the function truly appropriate to their specific natures.

5. Let us point out incidentally that this may oblige those still qualified for this path to 'take refuge', if one can speak thus, in organizations that practice other initiatic forms and that originally were not meant for them, a drawback that can be attenuated by certain 'adaptations' effected within these organizations.

6. The same is true of initiations such as that of the *Fedeli d'Amore*, as the very name clearly indicates, although the *jñānic* element seems to have been more developed than in chivalric initiation, with which it had close connections, moreover.

noted elsewhere, are a confirmation of what we said above about the impossibility of separating them completely. Later, the *bhaktic* forms disappeared, and the only initiations which continue to exist today in the West are the craft initiations, or what were such originally; even when, because of particular circumstances, the practice of a craft is no longer required as a necessary condition for initiation, which can only be regarded as a diminishment if not an actual degeneration, this changes nothing with regard to the essential character of these initiations.

Now, if the exclusive existence in the present-day West of initiatic forms that can be qualified as *karmic* is an incontestable fact, it still is necessary to say that the interpretations occasioned by this fact are not always exempt from ambiguities and confusions, and this from more than one point of view; this, then, is what remains to be examined in order for our exposition to be as complete as possible. First of all, some have imagined that, because of their *karmic* character, Western initiations are in some way opposed to those of the East, which, according to this point of view, would all be strictly *jñānic*.[7] This is wholly incorrect, for the truth is that in the East all categories of initiatic forms co-exist, as is sufficiently proved by the teaching of Hinduism on the three *mārgas*; if in the West, on the contrary, there no longer exists more than one, it is because the possibilities of that order have been reduced to a minimum. That the more and more exclusive predominance of the tendency to outer action is one of the principal causes of this situation is not in doubt; but it is no less true that despite the aggravation of this tendency, an initiation of some sort still exists, and to claim the contrary implies a serious misunderstanding of the real significance of the *karmic* path, as we shall soon see more precisely. Moreover, it is not admissible to want to turn what is only the effect of a single contingent situation into a question of principle, and to envisage things as if every Western initiatic form must necessarily be of the *karmic* type merely because it is Western. We believe there is no need to dwell further on this, for given everything we have said, it should be clear enough that such a

---

7. It should be noted that according to such a conception the existence of *bhaktic* initiations is completely unknown or neglected.

view cannot correspond to reality, which is obviously much more complex than it seems to suppose.

Another important point is this: the word *Karma*, when applied to a path or to an initiatic form, must be understood above all in its technical sense of 'ritual action'. In this regard it is easy to see that in every initiation there must be a certain *karmic* aspect, since it always essentially implies the accomplishment of particular rites; this also corresponds to what we said about the impossibility of any of the three paths existing in a pure state. Besides, and apart from rites properly speaking, every action, in order to be truly 'normal', that is to say conformable with 'order', must be 'ritualized', and, as we have often explained, each is effectively 'ritualized' in an integrally traditional civilization. Even in cases that one could call 'mixed', that is, where a certain degeneration has led to the introduction of the profane point of view and has allowed it a greater or lesser role in human activity, this still remains true at least for every action related to initiation, and it is notably so for everything having to do with the practice of a craft in the case of craft initiations.[8] It can be seen that this is as far as possible from the idea of a *karmic* path held by those who think that, because an initiatic organization presents a *karmic* character, it must involve itself more or less directly with an outer and wholly profane activity, as are inevitably in particular all 'social' activities in the conditions of the modern world. The reason invoked to support their conception is generally that such an organization has the duty to contribute to the well-being and betterment of humanity as a whole; this intention may be very praiseworthy in itself, but the way its realization is viewed remains no less erroneous, even if shorn of the 'progressivist' illusions too often associated with it. This is certainly not to say that an initiatic organization cannot propose for itself a secondary goal like those they have in mind, 'in addition' as it were, and on the condition that it never be confused with what constitutes its proper and essential goal; but then, to exercise an influence on its outer milieu without ceasing to be

---

8. One could say that in this case *karmic* is almost synonymous with 'operative', understanding this last word of course in its true sense which we have often emphasized.

what it must truly be, the organization must come up with wholly different means than those which such people doubtless believe to be the only ones possible, means that are much more 'subtle' but thereby only more efficacious. To claim the contrary is basically to misunderstand completely the value of what we have sometimes called an 'action of presence'; and this misunderstanding in the initiatic order is comparable to that regarding the role of the contemplative orders in the exoteric and religious framework also so widespread in our time; in the final analysis, both cases are a consequence of the same specifically modern mentality, for which everything that does not appear outwardly and that does not come under the senses is as if non-existent.

While we are on this subject, we shall add that there are also many misunderstandings on the nature of the two other paths, especially the *bhaktic* path, for, as regards the *jñānic* path, it is too difficult to confuse pure Knowledge, or even the traditional sciences that depend on it and that belong more properly to the domain of the 'lesser mysteries', with the speculations of philosophy and of profane science. By reason of its more strictly transcendent character, it is much easier to ignore this path completely than to denature it by false conceptions; and even the 'philosophical' travesties of certain orientalists, which retain absolutely nothing essential and reduce everything to the vain shadow-play of 'abstractions', are equivalent in fact to pure and simple ignorance and are too far removed from the truth to be able to give anyone the least notion of anything initiatic. As for *Bhakti*, the case is rather different, and here errors arise above all from a confusion of the initiatic sense of this term with its exoteric sense, which almost necessarily acquires in Western eyes a specifically religious and more or less 'mystical' aspect that it could never have in the Eastern traditions. This surely has nothing in common with initiation, and if it were really a question of nothing else, it is obvious that it could not constitute *Bhakti-Yoga*; but this leads us again to the question of mysticism and its essential differences with initiation.

19

ASCESIS
AND ASCETICISM

WE HAVE ON VARIOUS OCCASIONS noticed that some people make
an all too little justified connection between the terms 'ascetic' and
'mystical'. To dispel any confusion in this regard it is sufficient to
understand that the word 'ascesis' properly designates a methodical
effort to attain a certain goal, and more particularly a goal of a spiritual order,[1] whereas mysticism, as we have often said, by reason of
its passive character, implies rather the absence of any definite
method.[2] On the other hand, the word 'ascetic' has acquired a more
restricted meaning than that of 'ascesis', for it is applied almost
exclusively in the religious domain, and perhaps this explains to a
degree the confusion we speak of, for it goes without saying that
everything 'mystical' in the current acceptation of the word also
belongs to that same domain; but we must be careful not to think
that, conversely, everything of the religious order is thereby more or
less closely connected to mysticism, a strange error committed by
certain moderns, and, it is worth noting, especially by those who
are the most openly hostile to all religion.

1. Perhaps it is not useless to say that the word 'ascesis', which is of Greek origin,
has no etymological relationship with the Latin *ascendere*, for there are some who
let themselves be fooled in this regard by a purely and wholly accidental phonetic
similarity between these words. Moreover, even if ascesis aims at obtaining an
'ascension' of the being toward more or less elevated states, it is obvious that the
means can in no way be confounded with the result.

2. Cf. *Perspectives on Initiation*, chap. 1

There is another word derived from 'ascesis', that is, 'asceticism', which perhaps lends itself even more to confusions, for it has clearly been diverted from its original meaning to the point that, in current language, it has come to be hardly more than a synonym of 'austerity'. Now it is evident that most mystics devote themselves to austerities, sometimes even excessively, although they are not the only ones to do so, for this is a rather general characteristic of the 'religious life' as conceived in the West by virtue of the very widespread notion that suffering, especially voluntary suffering, has a value in itself; it is also certain that this notion, which has nothing in common with the original meaning of 'ascesis' and is in no way bound up with it, is generally even more particularly accentuated among mystics, though, let it be said again, it is far from being exclusive to them.[3] On the other hand—and this no doubt makes it understandable that 'asceticism' has acquired such a meaning—it is natural that all ascesis, or any rule of life directed to a spiritual goal, appears in the eyes of the 'worldly' to be clothed with an appearance of austerity, even if it in no way implies the idea of suffering, and quite simply because it is bound to dismiss or neglect the things that they themselves regard as the most important, if not even wholly essential, to human life, the pursuit of which fills their entire existence.

And yet in ordinary usage 'asceticism' seems to imply something else, something which should normally be only a preparatory means, but which is too often taken as an end; we believe we do not exaggerate in saying that for many religious minds asceticism does not aim at the effective realization of spiritual states, but is motivated solely by the hope for a 'salvation' that will only be reached in 'the other life'. We do not wish to belabor this point, but it does seem that in such a case the deviation no longer consists in the meaning of the word but in the very thing it designates; it is a deviation, let us say, certainly not because there would be something more or less illegitimate in the desire for 'salvation', but because a true 'ascesis' must have in view results that are more direct and more precise. Such results, to whatever degree they may go, are

3. Cf. ibid., chap. 25.

moreover, even in the exoteric and religious order, the true goal of the 'ascetic'. But how many are there nowadays who suspect that they can also be attained by an active life, thus one altogether different from the passive way of the mystics?

However that may be, the meaning of the word 'ascesis' itself, if not that of its derivatives, is sufficiently broad to apply to all orders and levels; since it is essentially a matter of a body of methodic practices leading to a spiritual development, one can very well speak not only of a religious ascesis but also of an initiatic ascesis. It is only necessary to note carefully that the goal of initiatic ascesis is not subject to any of the restrictions that almost by very definition necessarily limit that of religious ascesis, since the exoteric point of view to which the latter is joined relates exclusively to the individual human state,[4] whereas the initiatic point of view includes the realization of supra-individual states, up to the supreme and unconditioned state itself.[5] Furthermore, it goes without saying that the errors or deviations concerning ascesis that can occur in the religious domain cannot be found in the initiatic domain, for in the final analysis they only arise from the very limitations inherent to the exoteric point of view as such; what we have just said about asceticism in particular can obviously be explained only by the more or less narrowly restricted spiritual horizon of most men, who are exclusively exoterists and consequently 'religious' men in the most ordinary sense of the term.

The word 'ascesis' such as we understand it here is what in Western languages corresponds most closely to the Sanskrit *tapas*, and although it is true that this latter term conveys an idea not directly expressed by the Western term, this idea is no less plainly included

4. Of course the individuality is here envisaged in its integrality, with all the extensions of which it is susceptible, without which the religious idea of 'salvation' itself would really have no meaning at all.

5. It seems hardly necessary to recall that this is precisely the essential difference between 'salvation' and 'Deliverance'; not only are these two goals of different orders, but they do not even belong to orders that, although different, could still be comparable, since there can be no common measure between any conditioned state and the unconditioned state.

in one's notion of ascesis. The first meaning of *tapas* is in fact that of 'heat'. In the present case this heat is obviously that of an interior fire[6] that must consume what the Kabbalists would call the 'shells', that is to say it must in effect destroy everything within us that is an obstacle to spiritual realization; and so this indeed characterizes in the most general way all methods preparatory to such a realization, methods that from this point of view can be considered as constituting a 'purification' preliminary to the acquisition of any effective spiritual state.[7] If *tapas* often acquires the sense of a difficult or painful effort, this is not because a special value or importance is attributed to suffering as such, or because this latter may here be regarded as anything more than an 'accident', but because, by the very nature of things, detachment from contingencies is inevitably difficult for the individual, whose very existence also belongs to the contingent order. There is nothing here that could be assimilated to an 'expiation' or a 'penance', ideas which on the contrary play a large role in asceticism understood in the common way and which doubtless have their raison d'être in a certain aspect of the religious point of view, but which manifestly could not have any place in the initiatic domain, nor moreover in traditions not clothed in a religious form.[8]

Fundamentally, one could say that all true ascesis is essentially a 'sacrifice', and elsewhere we have had occasion to see that in all traditions sacrifice, whatever form it takes, properly constitutes the ritual act par excellence, that which as it were sums up all the others. What is thus gradually sacrificed in ascesis[9] are all the contingencies

---

6. The relation between this interior fire and the 'sulfur' of the Hermeticists, which is also conceived as a principle of an igneous nature, is too obvious to require more than passing notice (see *The Great Triad*, chap. 12).

7. This should be compared with what we have said concerning the true nature of spiritual trials (*Perspectives on Initiation*, chap. 25).

8. In translations by orientalists, one frequently encounters the words 'penance' and 'penitent', which really do not apply at all to what is involved, whereas 'ascesis' and 'ascetic' on the contrary would fit perfectly in most cases.

9. We say 'gradually' for the very reason that it is a matter of a methodical process, and it is easy to understand moreover that, save perhaps for certain exceptional cases, complete detachment cannot be achieved all at once.

from which a being must succeed in disengaging itself as from so many bonds or obstacles preventing it from rising to a higher state;[10] but if it can and must sacrifice these contingencies, this is insofar as they depend on and are somehow part of it.[11] Moreover, just as the individuality itself is but a contingency, ascesis, in its most complete and deepest meaning, is ultimately nothing other than the sacrifice of the 'ego', accomplished in order to realize a consciousness of the 'Self'.

10. For this being it can be said that these contingencies are thenceforth destroyed as such, that is, as manifested things, for they truly no longer exist for it, although subsisting without change for other beings; but this apparent destruction is in any case really a 'transformation', for it goes without saying that from the principial point of view nothing that is can ever be destroyed.

11. In this connection, one may recall the symbolism of the 'narrow gate' that cannot be entered by one who, like the 'rich man' of the Gospel, has not been able to divest himself of contingencies, or who 'having wished to save his soul [that is, his ego], loses it,' because in these conditions he cannot unite himself effectively with the permanent and immutable principle of his being.

20

GURU
AND *UPAGURU*

IF THE INITIATIC ROLE of the *guru* or spiritual master is often spoken of (which of course does not mean that those who speak of it
always understand it exactly), there is on the other hand another
notion that is generally passed over in silence: what the Hindu tradition designates by the word *upaguru*. This term must be understood to signify every being, whatever it may be, with whom an
encounter is for someone the occasion or starting-point of a spiritual development; and, in a general way, it is not at all necessary that
this being itself be conscious of the role it plays. Moreover, if we
speak here of a being, we could just as well speak also of a thing, or
even of some circumstance that brings about the same effect, which
finally comes back to what we have often said, namely that anything
at all can, according to the case, act as an 'occasional cause' in this
regard. It goes without saying that the latter is not a cause in the
strict sense of the word, and that in reality the true cause is found in
the very nature of the one upon whom this action is exercised, as is
shown by the fact that what has such an effect upon him may very
well have none at all upon another individual. And we might add
that *upagurus*, thus understood, can naturally be multiple in the
course of one and the same spiritual development, for each has only
a transitory role and can act effectively only at a certain determinate
moment, outside of which its intervention can have no more
importance than do most of the things that occur to us at every
instant and that we consider more or less indifferent.

The designation *upaguru* indicates that it has only an accessory
and subordinate role, which can be regarded as that of an auxiliary

to the true *guru*; indeed, the latter must know how to make use of all circumstances favorable to the development of his disciples, in conformity with the particular possibilities and aptitudes of each, and if he is truly a spiritual master in the complete sense of the word he may even sometimes himself provoke such circumstances at a desired moment. One could therefore say that in a certain way the *upagurus* are only 'prolongations' of the *guru* in the same way that the instruments and various means used by a being to exercise or amplify its action are so many prolongations of itself; and consequently it is evident that his proper role is in no way diminished thereby but, quite to the contrary, that he finds in them the possibility of acting more completely and in a way that is better adapted to the nature of each disciple, the indefinite diversity of contingent circumstances always permitting him to find in them some correspondence with that of their individual natures.

What we have just said applies to cases that can be considered normal, or that at least ought to be so with respect to the initiatic process, namely, cases implying the effective presence of a human *guru*. And before passing on to considerations of another order, equally applicable to the more or less exceptional cases that can in fact exist apart from the normal, it is appropriate to make another observation. When initiation properly speaking is conferred by someone who does not possess the qualities required to fulfill the function of a spiritual master, and who therefore acts solely as a 'transmitter' of the influence attached to the rite that he accomplishes, such an initiator may also be properly assimilated to an *upaguru*, which as such has a very particular and as it were unique importance of its kind, since it is its intervention that really determines the 'second birth', this being so even if the initiation is to remain merely virtual. This is also the only case where the *upaguru* must necessarily be conscious of his role, at least to some degree; we add this restriction because, when it is a matter of more or less degenerate or diminished initiatic organizations, it may happen that the initiator is ignorant of the true nature of what he transmits and even has no idea of the efficacy inherent in rites, which, as we have explained on other occasions, in no way prevents the latter from being valid as long as they are accomplished regularly and under the proper conditions. Only, it must be clearly understood that, lacking a *guru*, such an initiation runs a great risk of never becoming effective, except perhaps in certain exceptional cases that we may speak about at some other time; all that we will say for the moment is that, although theoretically there is no absolute impossibility in this, it is almost as rare in fact as is an initiatic affiliation obtained outside the ordinary means, so that it is hardly useful to consider it when limiting oneself to what is susceptible of the widest application.

Having said this, let us return to the consideration of *upagurus* in general, about which we must still clarify a more profound meaning than that we have indicated so far, for the human *guru* himself is basically only the exteriorized and as it were 'materialized' representation of the true 'inner *guru*', and need for him is due to the fact that the initiate, as long as he has not reached a certain degree of spiritual development, is incapable of entering directly into conscious communication with it. Whether or not there is a human *guru*, the inner *guru* is always present since it is one with the very 'Self'; and in the final analysis this is the point of view that one must adopt if one wishes to understand initiatic realities fully; moreover, in this respect there are no longer any exceptions like those to which we have just alluded, but only diverse modalities according to which this inner *guru* acts. Like the human *guru*, but to a lesser degree and more 'partially' so to speak, *upagurus* are its manifestations; as such they are, one could say, the appearances that it assumes in order to communicate in the measure possible with a being that cannot as yet relate to it directly, so that communication can only be effected by means of these 'exterior' supports. This allows us to understand why for example it is said that the old man, the sick man, the corpse, and the monk successively encountered by the future Buddha were forms taken by the *Devas* who wished to direct him toward illumination, these *Devas* themselves representing here only aspects of the inner *guru*; by this one need not necessarily understand that these were only 'apparitions', although assuredly these may also be possible in certain cases. The individual reality of the being that plays the role of an *upaguru* is in no way affected or destroyed thereby; if, however, it is in any way effaced before the reality of a higher order of which it is the occasional and momentary 'support', it is so only for the one to whom the 'message', of which consciously, or more often unconsciously, it has become the bearer, is especially addressed.

To prevent any misunderstanding, let us add that one must be very careful not to interpret what we have just said in the sense that the manifestations of the inner *guru* would only constitute something 'subjective'. This is not at all what we mean, and from our point of view 'subjectivity' is only the emptiest illusion. The higher reality of which we speak is situated well beyond the 'psychological' domain, at a level where the 'subjective' truly has no more meaning. Indeed, some may find this too evident to dwell upon, but we are only too familiar with the mentality of most of our contemporaries not to know that such precisions are far from being superfluous. Have we not encountered people who, when it is a question of the 'spiritual master', go so far as to render this term as 'director of conscience'?

21

TRUE AND FALSE
SPIRITUAL TEACHERS

WE HAVE OFTEN EMPHASIZED the distinction that should be made between initiation properly speaking, which is the pure and simple affiliation with an initiatic organization, implying essentially the transmission of a spiritual influence, and the means that can thereafter be used to make effective what at first was only virtual, means the efficacy of which is naturally subordinate in all cases to the indispensable condition of a prior affiliation. Insofar as they constitute an aid brought from without to the interior work from which the spiritual development of the being should result (and of course they can never take the place of this work itself), these means can in their totality be designated by the term initiatic teaching, taking this latter in its widest sense and not limiting it to the communication of certain ideas of a doctrinal order, but including in it everything that in one way or another is of a nature to guide the initiate in the work he is accomplishing to achieve spiritual realization of whatever degree.

What is most difficult, especially in our time, is certainly not obtaining an initiatic affiliation—which may sometimes be only too easy[1]—but finding an instructor who is truly qualified, that is, as we have just said, one really capable of discharging the function of a spiritual guide by applying all the suitable means to the disciple's

---

1. By this we wish to allude to the fact that certain initiatic organizations have become much too 'open', which is moreover always a cause of degeneration for them.

particular possibilities, apart from which it is clearly impossible, even for the most perfect master, to obtain any effective result. Without such an instructor, as we have already explained, the initiation remains merely virtual save for rare exceptions, although it is certainly valid in itself from the time that the spiritual influence has really been transmitted by means of the appropriate rite.[2] What further aggravates the difficulty is that those who claim to be spiritual guides without being at all qualified for this role, have probably never been as numerous as they are today, and the resulting danger is all the greater because in fact these people generally have very powerful and more or less abnormal psychic powers, which obviously prove nothing from the point of view of spiritual development and in this respect are ordinarily even rather an unfavorable indication, but which are nonetheless capable of creating an illusion and imposing it on all who are insufficiently informed and consequently cannot make the essential distinctions. Therefore, one cannot be too much on guard against such false teachers, who can only lead astray those who let themselves be seduced by them, and who ought to consider themselves fortunate if they suffer nothing more than a waste of their time. Moreover, whether they be mere charlatans, of which there are only too many at present, or whether they delude themselves before deluding others, it goes without saying that this changes nothing as to the results, and in a certain way those who are more or less sincere (for there can be many degrees here) are perhaps even the more dangerous for their very unconsciousness. We hardly need add that the confusion of the psychic with the spiritual, unfortunately so widespread among our contemporaries, and which we have often denounced, greatly contributes to render possible the worst misunderstandings in this regard; and when one adds to this the attraction of alleged 'powers' and a taste for extraordinary 'phenomena', which moreover almost inevitably go together, one has a fairly complete explanation for the success of certain false teachers.

---

2. We must recall here that the initiator who acts as a 'transmitter' of the influence attached to the rite is not necessarily fit to play the role of teacher; if the two functions are normally combined where traditional institutions have suffered no diminution, they are in fact far from always being so in present-day conditions.

There is nonetheless a characteristic by which many if not all such false teachers can be easily recognized, and although this is only a direct and necessary consequence of what we have persistently said on the subject of initiation, we believe that, given questions that have been posed to us recently concerning various more or less suspect personages, it will not be useless to state it again more explicitly. Whoever presents himself as a spiritual teacher without attaching himself to a definite traditional form, or without conforming to the rules established by the latter, cannot truly possess the qualifications he attributes to himself; according to the case, he may either be a common imposter or a 'deluded' person ignorant of the real conditions of initiation, and in this latter case even more than in the former it is greatly to be feared that he is only too often nothing more than an instrument in the service of something that he himself may not suspect. We can say as much of anyone who claims to dispense indiscriminately an initiatic teaching to all, even to the merely profane, and who neglects as the first condition of its efficacy the need of affiliation with a regular initiatic organization; or again, of anyone who proceeds according to methods that do not conform to those of any traditionally recognized initiation (moreover, these cases are identical to the first up to a point). If one knows how to apply these few indications and always holds strictly to them, the promoters of 'pseudo-initiations', of whatever cast, would find themselves almost immediately unmasked;[3] only the danger that can come from deviant, though real, initiations that have departed from the line of traditional orthodoxy, would still remain; but such cases are certainly much less prevalent, at least in the Western world, so that it is clearly much less urgent to worry about them in the present circumstances. Furthermore, we can at the very least say that the 'teachers' affiliated with such initiations, in common with the others we have mentioned, generally share the habit of

---

3. As we have explained on other occasions, one must naturally not forget to count among the 'pseudo-initiations' all that claim to base themselves on traditional forms that no longer have any effective existence; the former at least are clearly recognizable at first sight, and without there being any need to examine things more closely, whereas this may not always be the case for the latter.

showing off their psychic 'powers' at every opportunity and without any valid reason (for we cannot consider valid the desire to attract disciples or to retain them by such means, which is the end they usually have in mind), and attribute the preponderance of such displays to an excessive and more or less disordered development of possibilities of that order, something that is always detrimental to any true spiritual development.

As for true spiritual teachers on the other hand, the contrast they strike with false teachers in the different respects we have just noted, can make them, if not recognizable with complete certainty (in the sense that these conditions, although necessary, can nonetheless be insufficient), at least help greatly to that end. But here it is appropriate to make another remark in order to dispel other false ideas. Contrary to what many people seem to imagine, it is not always necessary that, in order to be able to fulfill this role within certain limits, someone must himself have arrived at a complete spiritual realization; indeed, it should be quite evident that much less than this is required to be capable of guiding a disciple validly through the first stages of his initiatic journey. Of course, once the disciple has reached the point beyond which the former cannot guide him, the teacher worthy of the name will never hesitate to let him know that henceforth he can do no more for him, and in order that he may continue his work in the most favorable conditions, direct him either to his own master, if this is possible, or to another teacher whom he recognizes as more completely qualified than himself; and when this is the case, there is really nothing astonishing or even abnormal in that disciple's finally surpassing the spiritual level of his first teacher, who, if he is truly what he ought to be, will be satisfied to have contributed his part, however modest it may be, in leading his former disciple to this result. Indeed, individual jealousies and rivalries can find no place in the true initiatic domain, whereas, on the contrary, they almost always play a very great part in the actions of false teachers; and it is solely these latter who should be fought and denounced whenever circumstances require, not only by authentic spiritual masters, but also by all who are to any degree conscious of what initiation really is.

22

INNATE WISDOM
AND ACQUIRED WISDOM

CONFUCIUS taught that there are two kinds of sage, those who are so by birth and others, among whom he counted himself, who become so only through their own efforts; and it should be remembered that, as he understood it, the 'sage' (*cheng*), who represents the highest degree of the Confucian hierarchy, also constitutes the first level of the Taoist hierarchy, thus occupying the limit as it were where the exoteric and esoteric domains meet, as we have already explained elsewhere.[1] Given these conditions it can be asked if, when he speaks of the sage by birth, Confucius only meant to designate the man who by nature possesses all the qualifications required to attain the initiatic hierarchy effectively and without further preparation, and who consequently has no need at the start to endeavor to climb little by little, by more or less long and arduous studies, the grades of the exterior hierarchy. This interpretation is indeed very possible—even the most likely—and is all the more legitimate in that at the very least it implies the recognition that there are beings destined so to speak by their own possibilities to pass immediately beyond the exoteric domain where Confucius himself always meant to remain. On the other hand, however, it can also be asked if, by passing beyond the limitations inherent in the strictly Confucian point of view, innate wisdom is not susceptible of a wider and deeper meaning, of which the other we have just noted could be considered a particular case.

---

1. *The Great Triad*, chap. 18.

It is easy to understand how such a question should arise, for as we have often had occasion to say, all effective knowledge constitutes a permanent acquisition that a being obtains once and for all and that nothing can ever take away. Consequently, if a being that has reached a certain degree of realization in one state of existence should pass on to another state, it would necessarily take along what it had acquired, which would thus appear as 'innate' in its new state; and besides, this could only be the case with a realization that has remained incomplete, for otherwise the passage to another state would have no conceivable meaning; and when a being passes on to the human state—the case that particularly interests us here— realization cannot have reached the point of liberation from the conditions of individual existence, but it can extend from the most elementary stages to the point nearest that which, in the human state, corresponds to the perfection of this state.[2] It could even be pointed out that in the primordial state all beings born as men must have been in this latter situation, since they possessed this perfection of their individuality in a natural and spontaneous way, without having to make any effort to attain it, and this implies that they were at the point of attaining it before being born into the human state. They were thus truly sages by birth, and this not only in the restricted sense inherent in the Confucian point of view, but in all the fullness of meaning that can be given to this expression.

Before going further it would be well to call attention to the fact that here we are speaking of something acquired in states of existence other than the human, something which therefore has and can have nothing in common with any 'reincarnationist' concept whatsoever; moreover, besides all the reasons of a metaphysical order that absolutely prevent this in any case, such a conception would be even more manifestly absurd in the case of the first men, which makes it useless to dwell further on the matter. What is perhaps more important to stress here, since it is more easily misunderstood, is that when we speak of the human state, this anteriority must not

---

2. We say only the nearest point because, if the perfection of an individual state had indeed been effectively attained, such a being would no longer have to pass to another individual state.

be conceived literally as a succession more or less assimilable to temporal succession such as it exists within the human state itself, but only as expressing the causal sequence of the different states; these latter can in truth only be described as successive in a purely symbolic way, but it goes without saying that, without recourse to a symbolism conforming to the conditions of our world, it would be altogether impossible in any case to express things intelligibly in human language. With this reservation, one can speak of a being as having attained a certain degree of realization before its birth into the human state; it suffices to know in what sense this is to be understood in order that this way of speaking, inadequate as it may be in itself, present no real inconvenience; and it is thus that such a being will possess from birth the degree corresponding to this realization in the human world, a degree that can extend from that of *cheng* or Confucian sage, up to that of *chen jen* or 'true man'.

It must not be believed however that in the present conditions of the terrestrial world this innate wisdom can manifest itself in a wholly spontaneous way, as was the case in the primordial age, for it is obviously necessary to take into account the obstacles posed by the environment. Such a being must therefore have recourse to the means that in fact exist for surmounting these obstacles, which amounts to saying that it is in no way exempt, as one might be tempted to incorrectly suppose, from affiliation with an initiatic 'chain', failing which, so long as it is in the human state, it will remain what it was upon entering therein, and as if plunged into a sort of spiritual 'sleep' that does not permit it to go further on its path of realization. It is even conceivable that, if need be, it should outwardly manifest the state of *cheng jen* without having to develop it gradually, because this latter is still only at the upper limit of the exoteric domain; but for everything that is beyond this, initiation properly speaking always constitutes an indispensable condition at present, and is moreover sufficient in such a case.[3] This being may then appear to pass through the same stages as the initiate who has

3. The only case where this condition does not exist is that of descending realization, for this presupposes that the ascending realization has been accomplished

merely started from the state of the ordinary man, but the reality will be quite different. Indeed, not only will the initiation be immediately effective for it, instead of initially being virtual as is usually the case, but the being will still 'recognize' these stages, if one may so express it, as already existing within it, in a way that can be compared to Platonic 'reminiscence', which in fact is doubtless one of the meanings of this latter. This case is also comparable, in the order of theoretical knowledge, to that of someone who already possesses the consciousness of certain doctrinal truths inwardly, but who is incapable of expressing them because he does not have the appropriate terms at his disposal, and who, once he hears these terms uttered, immediately recognizes them and wholly penetrates their meaning without needing any effort to assimilate them. It can even happen that upon finding himself in the presence of initiatic rites and symbols, these latter should appear to him as if he had always known them in an as it were 'intemporal' way, because he effectively has within himself everything that, beyond and independent of particular forms, constitutes their very essence; and in fact this 'knowledge' has no temporal beginning since it results from an acquisition realized outside the course of the human state, which alone is truly conditioned by time.

Another consequence of what we have just said is that in order to traverse the initiatic path a man such as this has no need of an outer and human *guru*, since in reality the true inner *guru* acts in him from the beginning, obviously making the intervention of any provisional 'substitute' superfluous, for the role of the outer *guru* is after all nothing other than this; and this is the exceptional case to which we have already alluded.[4] What must be clearly understood however is precisely that this case can only be altogether exceptional, and is all the more exceptional to the degree that humanity moves further along the descending path of its cycle; indeed, it can be viewed as something of a last vestige of the primordial state and of those who followed it prior to the *Kali-Yuga*, a vestige moreover

---

to its ultimate term; obviously, this is then completely different from the case we are presently considering.

4. In chapter 20. Ed.

that is bound to be hidden, since the man who possesses 'by right' and from his birth the quality of 'true man', or what corresponds to a lesser degree of realization, can in fact no longer develop in a wholly spontaneous way, independent of any contingent circumstances. Of course, for him the role of contingencies is still reduced to the minimum, since it is purely and simply a question of initiatic affiliation, which it is obviously always possible for him to obtain, all the more in that he will be as if invincibly drawn to it by the 'affinities' that are an effect of his very nature. But what must be avoided above all, for it is always a danger to be feared when considering exceptions like these, is that some people will too easily imagine that such is their own case, either because they feel themselves naturally inclined to seek initiation—which usually only indicates that they are ready to enter this path, and not that they have already partially traversed it in another state—or because, before any initiation, that they had a few more or less vague 'glimmers', probably of an order more psychic than spiritual, which, after all, are no more extraordinary and prove nothing more than do the commonplace 'premonitions' that anyone whose faculties are a bit less narrowly limited than are commonly those of present-day humanity might occasionally have, and which are therefore less exclusively enclosed in the corporeal mode of his individuality; this moreover, generally speaking, does not even necessarily imply that the individual in question is really qualified for initiation. All of these assuredly represent reasons are altogether insufficient for claiming to be able to dispense with a spiritual master and arrive nonetheless surely at effective initiation, any more than for dispensing with all personal effort in view of this result. The truth obliges us to say that this is a possibility that exists, but also that it can belong only to a tiny minority, so much so that in practical terms there is finally no need to take it into account. Those who really possess this possibility will always become conscious of it at the desired moment in a certain and indubitable way, and ultimately this is the only thing that matters; as for the others, if they let themselves be drawn in, put their faith in vain fantasies, and act accordingly, this can only lead to the most unfortunate deceptions.

23

COLLECTIVE INITIATIC
WORK AND SPIRITUAL
'PRESENCE'

THERE ARE INITIATIC FORMS in which, by their very constitution, collective work holds as it were a preponderant place; we do not of course mean that this could ever substitute for each member's personal and purely interior work, or that this latter could in any way be dispensed with, but it at least constitutes an essential element in such a case, whereas its role can be limited or even wholly lacking elsewhere. This is particularly true of initiations found in the West today, and no doubt it is generally the same to a greater or lesser degree in all craft initiations wherever these are found, for collective work appears to be something inherent to their very nature. This is related for example to the fact, to which we alluded in a recent study on Masonry,[1] of a 'communication' that can only be effected through the cooperation of three persons, none of whom alone possesses the power necessary for this result; and in the same order of ideas we can also cite the condition that a certain minimum number of participants, seven, for example, be present in order to ensure a valid initiation, whereas there are other initiations, frequently met with in India, where the transmission is effected simply from master to disciple, without the cooperation of anyone else. It goes without saying that such a difference in modalities must entail equally

---

1. See 'Parole Perdue et Mots Substitués' in the December 1948 issue of *Études Traditionnelles* [included as 'Lost Word & Substituted Words' in *Studies in Freemasonry and the Compagnonnage*].

different consequences throughout all the later initiatic work; and among these consequences we are especially interested in examining more closely those relating to the role of the *guru* or of what takes his place.

In the case of initiatic transmission effected by a single person, the latter thereby assumes the function of *guru* toward the initiate; and it matters little whether his qualifications in this regard be more or less complete, or whether, as often happens, he is only capable of leading his disciple to a certain determined stage, for the principle is always the same: the *guru* is present from the beginning and there can be no doubt as to his identity. The collective situation, on the contrary, is much less simple and less obvious, and one can legitimately ask where the *guru* really is; no doubt, when any 'master' instructs an 'apprentice' he takes the *guru's* place in a certain sense and to a certain degree, but only in a very relative fashion, and even if the one who effects the initiatic transmission is properly speaking only an *upaguru*, all the others will also be so, and with all the more reason; besides, there is nothing here resembling the exclusive relationship of the disciple with a single *guru*, which is an indispensable condition for using this term in its true sense. In such initiations it does not in fact appear that there have ever been any spiritual masters properly speaking who have exercised their function in a continuous way; if there have been such, which is a possibility we cannot exclude,[2] this has been an exception, and their presence has not been a constant and necessary element in the special constitution of the initiatic forms in question. However, there must in spite of everything be something that takes their place, which is why one must ask who or what has effectively filled this function in such cases.

One might be tempted to answer this question by saying that here it is the collectivity itself, composed of the initiatic organization as a whole, that plays the role of *guru*, an answer in fact suggested quite naturally by the remark we made at the beginning

2. There must necessarily have been such masters, at least at the origin of every distinct initiatic form, for only they could have been qualified to effect the 'adaptation' required to establish it.

about the preponderant importance then accorded to the collective work; but without saying that this is entirely false, it is at least wholly inadequate. Moreover, it is necessary to make very clear that when we speak in this respect of a collectivity we do not mean merely a gathering of individuals considered in their corporeal modality alone, as could be the case of any profane group; what we have particularly in mind is the collective 'psychic entity', to which some have given the very inappropriate name 'egregore'. Let us recall what we have already said in this connection:[3] the 'collective' as such can never transcend the individual domain since in the final analysis it is only a resultant of the component individualities, nor, consequently, can it go beyond the psychic order; now all that is only psychic can have no effective and direct relationship with initiation since this latter consists essentially in the transmission of a spiritual influence meant to produce effects of a similar spiritual order, thus transcendent with respect to the individuality, whence one obviously must conclude that whatever is able to render effective the initially virtual action of this influence, must itself necessarily have a supra-individual and thus, if one may put it so, a supra-collective character. Moreover, it is evident that it is not as an individual human being that the *guru* properly speaking exercises his function, but insofar as he represents something supra-individual, of which, in respect of this function, his individuality is in reality only a support; thus in order for the two cases to be comparable, it is necessary that what is here assimilable to the *guru's* not be the collectivity itself but the transcendent principle for which it serves as support and which alone confers on it a true initiatic character. What is involved therefore can be called in the strictest sense of the word a spiritual 'presence', acting in and by the collective work itself; and it is the nature of this 'presence' that we must now explain somewhat more completely, though without claiming to treat the question in all its aspects.

In the Hebrew Kabbalah it is said that when the sages converse about the divine mysteries, the *Shekinah* is present among them; thus, even in an initiatic form where the collective work does not in

3. See chapter 6, 'Spiritual Influences and "Egregores"'.

general seem to be an essential element, a spiritual 'presence' is no less clearly averred when such a work takes place, and it can be said that this 'presence' manifests itself at the intersection as it were of the 'lines of force' running between those participating in it, as if its 'descent' were directly invoked by the resulting collective produced at this determinate point, which furnishes it with the appropriate support. We will not dwell further on this perhaps somewhat overly 'technical' aspect of the question, adding only that here it is a matter of the work of initiates who have already reached an advanced degree of spiritual development, in contrast to that of organizations where the collective work constitutes the usual and normal modality from the very beginning; but of course this difference changes nothing as to the principle itself of the spiritual 'presence'.

What we have just said should be compared to this saying of Christ: 'When two or three are come together in my name, I am in their midst'; and this comparison is particularly striking when one knows the close connection between the Messiah and the *Shekinah*.[4] It is true that according to the current interpretation, this passage simply refers to prayer; but as legitimate as this application may be in the exoteric order, there is no reason to limit oneself to it exclusively and not also to envisage another, deeper meaning, which by this very fact will be true *a fortiori*; or at least there is no other reason for this except the limitation of the exoteric point of view itself, for those who cannot or will not go beyond it. We must also draw particular attention to the expression 'in my name', which moreover is so often encountered in the Gospel, for at present it seems to be

---

4. It is sometimes claimed that there existed a variant of this text in which 'three' are spoken of, rather than 'two or three', and some wish to interpret these three as the body, soul, and spirit; it would thus be a matter of concentrating and unifying all the elements of the being in the interior work necessary for the 'descent' of the spiritual influence at the center of the being to be operated. This interpretation is certainly plausible, and independent of the question of exactly which text is the more correct, it expresses in itself an incontestable truth, although without in any way excluding the truth related to the collective work; however, if the number three really was specified, one would have to admit that it then represents a minimum number required for the effectiveness of this work, as in fact it is in certain initiatic forms.

understood only in a greatly diminished sense, if in fact it does not pass unnoticed; almost no one any longer understands all that it really implies traditionally, both as to doctrine and ritual. We have already said a little about this last question on various occasions and will perhaps return to it again, but at the moment we only wish to point out a consequence that from our point of view is very important: in all strictness, the work of an initiatic organization must always be accomplished 'in the name' of the spiritual principle from which it proceeds and which it is destined as it were to manifest in some way in our world.[5] This principle can be more or less 'specialized' in conformity with the modalities proper to each initiatic organization; but, being of a purely spiritual nature as obviously required by the very goal of all initiatic organizations, it is in the final analysis always the expression of a divine aspect, and it is a direct emanation from this aspect that properly constitutes the inspiring and guiding 'presence' of the collective initiatic work, in order that this latter might produce effective results according to the measure of the capacities of each of those taking part in it.

---

5. Any ritual formula which does not correspond to what we have been describing, when substituted for this, can only represent a diminishment of it due to a misunderstanding or to a more or less complete ignorance of what the 'name' truly is, implying in consequence a certain degeneration of the initiatic organization, since this substitution shows that the latter is no longer fully conscious of the real nature of the relationship uniting it to its spiritual principle.

24

THE ROLE
OF THE *GURU*

WE HAVE RECENTLY had occasion to note such misapprehensions and exaggerations concerning the role of the *guru*[1] that we feel obliged to return to the question in order to somewhat rectify matters. In the presence of some of these assertions we are almost tempted to regret having emphasized this role as much as we have so frequently done; and while it is true that many people tend to deprecate the importance of the *guru*, if not to misunderstand it entirely (which is what justified our emphasis), it is now a matter of the opposite error.

There are those, then, who go so far as to claim that no one can attain Deliverance without the help of a *guru*, by which they naturally mean a human *guru*, to which we immediately respond that these people would assuredly do much better to concern themselves with matters less remote from them than the ultimate goal of spiritual realization, and to rest content with considering the question in reference to the first steps toward this realization, for which in fact the presence of a *guru* is especially necessary. As we have said before, it must not be forgotten that the human *guru* is in reality only an outer representative and a 'substitute', as it were, of the true inner *guru*, and that he is necessary only due to the fact that the initiate has not yet reached a certain degree of spiritual development and so is still incapable of entering directly into conscious communication

---

1. Although this term belongs properly to the Hindu tradition, for simplicity's sake we will understand it to mean a spiritual master in the most general sense, whatever his traditional form.

with the latter. That, in any case, is what limits the necessity for a human *guru* to the first stages, and we say 'first stages' because the communication in question obviously becomes possible for a being well before the point of attaining Deliverance. Now with this qualification in mind, must one consider this necessity absolute, or, in other words, is the presence of a human *guru* strictly indispensable in all cases at the beginning of realization, that is, indispensable not only to confer a valid initiation (for to deny this would be too obviously absurd) but to render effective an initiation which, without it, would remain merely virtual? As important as the role of the *guru* may really be—and it is not we who would dream of disputing it— we are obliged to say that such an assertion is altogether false for several reasons, the first of which is that there are exceptional cases of beings for whom a pure and simple initiatic transmission, without any intervention whatsoever by a *guru*, suffices to immediately 'awaken' the spiritual acquisitions obtained in other states of existence; as rare as these cases may be, they prove at the very least that this is in no way a necessity of principle. But here we have something more important to consider since it is no longer a question of exceptions that one could reasonably say need not be taken into account practically, but rather perfectly normal paths: there exist forms of initiation that by their very constitution do not require that anyone fulfill the function of *guru* in the strict sense of the word, and this is especially true of certain forms where collective work takes a preponderant place, the role of the *guru* then being played not by a human individual but by a spiritual influence that is effectively present in the course of this work.[2] No doubt this has a certain disadvantage, in the sense that such a path is obviously less

---

2. It is to be noted here that even in certain initiatic forms where the function of *guru* normally exists, it is nonetheless not always strictly indispensable in fact; thus, in Islamic initiation, certain *ṭuruq*, especially under present-day conditions, are no longer directed by a true Shaykh capable of effectively fulfilling the role of spiritual master, but only by *Khulafāʾ*, who can scarcely do more than validly transmit the initiatic influence; it is nonetheless true that in such a case the *barakah* of the Shaykh who founded the *ṭarīqah* can, at least for particularly well-endowed individuals, and simply by virtue of affiliation with the *silsilah*, make up for the absence of a presently living Shaykh, this case then becoming quite comparable to that we have just recalled.

sure and more difficult to follow than that where the initiate bene-
fits from the constant supervision of a spiritual master; but this is a
different question altogether, and what is important from our
present point of view is that the very existence of these initiatic
forms, which necessarily offer the same goal as the others, and
which consequently must offer their adherents means sufficient to
reach it, provided only that they are fully qualified, amply proves
that the presence of a *guru* need not be regarded as constituting an
indispensable condition in all cases. And of course, whether or not
there is a human *guru*, the inner *guru* is always present, since it is
one with the very 'Self'; whether, in order to manifest itself to those
who are not yet capable of having an immediate consciousness of it,
it takes as support a human being or a 'non-incarnated' spiritual
influence is, in the final analysis, only a difference of modality that
changes nothing essential.

We have just said that where it exists, the role of *guru* is especially
important at the beginning of the effective initiation, which might
seem perfectly obvious since it is natural that an initiate should have
more need of guidance the less he is advanced on the path; and this
remark already implicitly refutes another error we have noticed,
which consists in the claim that there is no true *guru* but the one
who has already reached the goal of spiritual realization, that is,
Deliverance. If this were really so it would be rather discouraging
for those seeking to obtain the help of a *guru*, for it is quite clear
that their chances of meeting one would be extremely slim; but in
order to fulfill the role of a *guru* effectively at the beginning, it is in
fact enough to be able to lead the disciple to a certain degree of
effective initiation, which is possible even if the one fulfilling this
role has not himself gone beyond that degree.[3] This is why the
ambition of a true *guru*, if one may put it so, must be above all
to bring his disciple as soon as possible to a position where he can
do without him, whether by sending the disciple, when he can no

---

3. In addition to the spiritual development corresponding to this degree, this
capacity also presupposes certain special qualifications, just as, among those possessing the same degree of any kind of knowledge, all are not equally able to teach it
to others.

longer lead him any further, to another *guru* whose competence exceeds his own[4] or, if he is able, by leading him to the point where a direct and conscious communication with the inner *guru* will be established; and in the latter case, this will be equally true whether the human *guru* is truly a *jivan-mukta* or possesses only a lesser degree of spiritual realization.

We have not yet finished with all the erroneous conceptions current in certain circles, among which is one that seems to us especially dangerous: there are those who imagine that they can consider themselves affiliated with some traditional form by the mere fact that their *guru*, or at least the one they feel justified in regarding as such, belongs to it, and without having to do anything else, or accomplish any rite whatsoever. It should be quite obvious that this claimed affiliation can have no real value, and that it does not even have the slightest reality; indeed, it would be too easy to attach oneself to a tradition if there were no other condition than this, and such an error can only be the effect of a complete failure to recognize the necessity of the practice of an exoterism, which, in the case of an initiation arising from a definite tradition that is not exclusively esoteric, must naturally belong to the same tradition as the initiation.[5] Those who hold such a view doubtless believe that they have passed beyond forms, but then their error is all the greater, for the very need they feel to resort to a *guru* sufficiently proves that they have not yet reached that point;[6] whether or not

---

4. Such a change is of course never regular and legitimate except with the authorization of the first *guru*, and even at his initiative, for he alone—and not the disciple—can judge whether his role vis-à-vis the latter is at an end, and also whether some other particular *guru* will really be capable of leading him further than he himself was able to do. Let us add that such a change can also sometimes have a very different motive, and be due simply to the fact that the *guru* sees that the disciple, by virtue of certain particularities of his individual nature, can be guided more effectively by someone else.

5. Here we take the word 'exoterism' in its broadest meaning, as designating the part of a tradition that addresses itself to everyone without distinction, and that constitutes the normal and necessary basis for every corresponding initiation.

6. There is even something contradictory here, for if they could really have reached this point before having a *guru*, that would certainly be the best proof that the latter is not indispensable, as they on the other hand assert him to be.

the *guru* himself has arrived there changes nothing regarding his disciples and in no way concerns them. It must be said that what is most astonishing is that there could be a *guru* who would accept disciples under such conditions and without first having rectified their error; even this alone would be of a nature to cause serious doubts as to the reality of his spiritual quality. Indeed, every true spiritual master must necessarily exercise his function in conformity with a definite tradition. When it is not so, this is one mark by which we may most easily recognize a false spiritual master, who in some cases may not indeed be acting in bad faith, but only deluding himself through ignorance of the real conditions of initiation, something we have already explained sufficiently[7] so that we need not dwell further on it. To forestall all objections, it is important to make a clear distinction between this case and that in which a spiritual master may, accidentally as it were and outside his traditional function, give to persons not of his own tradition not only doctrinal clarifications, which would raise no difficulties, but also more practical counsels; and it must be well understood that what is involved in such a case are only simple counsels, which, like those given by anyone else, take their value solely from the knowledge that the one who gives them possesses as a human individual and not as the representative of a certain tradition, and can never make the one who receives them a disciple of his in the initiatic sense of the word. This obviously has nothing in common with the claim to be able to confer an initiation on persons who do not fulfill the required conditions for receiving it validly, conditions among which are always and necessarily the regular and effective affiliation with the tradition to which the initiatic form in question belongs, with all the ritual observances that are essentially implied; and we must clearly state that without this affiliation the relationship uniting the so-called disciples to their *guru* is, as an initiatic bond, an illusion pure and simple.

7. See chapter 21, 'True and False Spiritual Teachers'.

25

ON THE
INITIATIC DEGREES

WE WERE GREATLY ASTONISHED to note recently that certain people, who should have had a better understanding of our repeated
explanations of initiation, were still committing rather strange
errors concerning this subject, bearing witness to altogether inaccu-
rate notions on questions that are after all relatively simple. Thus we
have heard the assertion—perfectly inexplicable coming from anyone who possesses, or ought to possess, some knowledge of these
things—that between the spiritual state of an initiate who has simply 'entered the path' and the 'primordial state' there is no intermediate degree. The truth is that on the contrary a great number of
such degrees exist, for the path of the 'lesser mysteries', which leads
to the 'primordial state', takes very long to travel, and in fact few ever
reach its end; how then could anyone maintain that all who travel
this path are really at the same point, and that there are none who
have reached different stages? Besides, if such were the case, how
could it be that the initiatic forms related to the 'lesser mysteries'
generally include a plurality of degrees (three in some, seven in
others, to mention only the best known examples), and to what
could these degrees correspond? We have also cited a Taoist enu-
meration in which mention is made of two intermediate degrees
between the state of the 'wise man' and that of the 'true man';[1] and
this is a particularly clear example, since the 'primordial state'
(which is that of the 'true man') is expressly situated at the fourth

1. See *The Great Triad*, chap. 18.

degree of an initiatic hierarchy. Regardless of the way they are distributed, these degrees always represent (theoretically at least, or symbolically in cases involving a merely virtual initiation) nothing less than the different stages of an effective initiation, to which there necessarily correspond the same number of distinct spiritual states, of which they are the successive realizations; were it otherwise, they would be entirely devoid of any meaning. In reality, the intermediate degrees of initiation can even be indefinitely multiple, and it must be well understood that the degrees found in an initiatic organization never constitute anything but a more or less general and 'schematic' classification, limited to the consideration of certain principal stages, or those that are more sharply characterized—which moreover explains the diversity of these classifications.[2] Also, it goes without saying that even if for reasons of 'method' an initiatic organization does not confer degrees that are clearly distinct and marked by specific rites, this does not prevent the same stages from necessarily existing for those who are attached to them (at least as soon as they pass to effective initiation), for there are no means that allow one to attain the goal directly.

We can present the matter in another way, which will perhaps render it more 'tangible'. We have explained that initiation into the 'lesser mysteries', which naturally takes man such as he is in his present state, requires him to retrace as it were the cycle traversed in a descending direction by humanity as a whole in the course of its history, in order to lead him back finally to the 'primordial state' itself.[3] Now it is evident that between this latter state and the present state of humanity there have been many intermediate stages, as is proven by the traditional distinction of the four ages, each of which can be further subdivided; and since the spiritual degeneration was not accomplished at a single stroke but in successive stages, then logically regeneration cannot occur except by passing through the same stages in reverse sequence, thereby gradually approaching the 'primordial state' that is to be regained.

2. See *Perspectives on Initiation*, chap. 44.
3. Ibid., chap. 39.

We can better understand how some might believe that there are no distinct degrees on the path of the 'greater mysteries'—the path, that is, between the state of 'true man' and that of 'transcendent man'—for although such a belief is equally false, it is at least a more readily explicable illusion. There are however multiple supra-individual states, among which are some that are in reality very far from the unconditioned state in which alone is realized 'Deliverance' or the 'Supreme Identity'; but as soon as a being has passed beyond the 'primordial state' to any supra-individual state, those still in the individual human state lose sight of that being, as it were, just as an observer whose view is limited to a horizontal plane would know of a vertical only at its single point of intersection with that plane, all its other points necessarily escaping him. This point, which properly corresponds to the 'primordial state', is thus at the same time the sole 'trace' of all the supra-human states, as we have said elsewhere; that is why, from the human state, the 'transcendent man', along with all who have only realized supra-individual states that remain conditioned, are truly 'indistinguishable' from one another, which is also true of the 'true man' himself, who has however only reached the center of the human state and is not in effective possession of any superior state.[4]

These remarks have had no other purpose than to recall certain notions that we have previously explained, but that have apparently not always been sufficiently understood; and we thought it all the more necessary to return to them because it is truly dangerous for those who are still only at the first stage of initiation to imagine that they are already immediate candidates (if we may so express it) for the realization of the 'primordial state'. It is true that some go even further and are persuaded that, to obtain 'Deliverance' itself immediately, it is enough to experience a sincere desire accompanied by absolute confidence in a *guru*, without having to make the least effort oneself. In the presence of such aberrations one cannot but think that one is surely dreaming!

4. See *The Great Triad*, chap. 18.

26

AGAINST
QUIETISM

ALTHOUGH WE HAVE OFTEN SPOKEN already of the profound differences that separate mysticism from everything of an initiatic and esoteric order, we do not believe it unprofitable to return to a particular point relating to this question, as we have noticed that a widespread error persists which concerns the application of the word 'quietism' to certain Eastern doctrines. That this is already an error results from the fact that these doctrines have nothing to do with mysticism, whereas the very word 'quietism' was specifically coined to designate a form of mysticism, of a type moreover that can be called 'aberrant', and of which the principal characteristic is to push to an extreme the passivity that in one degree or another inheres in mysticism as such. Now on the one hand words of this sort must not be extended to what does not pertain to the domain of mysticism, for they then become just as improper as philosophical labels applied outside of philosophy; and on the other hand, passivity, even within the limits considered 'normal' as it were from the mystical point of view—and all the more in its 'Quietist' exaggeration—is altogether foreign to the doctrines in question. To tell the truth, we suspect that the imputation of 'quietism', like that of 'pantheism', is for some very often only a pretext for dismissing or disparaging a doctrine without taking the trouble to examine it more profoundly and really seeking to understand it. More generally, this is the case with all the 'pejorative' epithets they use without rhyme or reason to describe very different doctrines, reproaching them for 'falling' into this or that, an habitual expression in such cases and one that is very significant in this respect; but as we have noted on other occasions, every error necessarily occurs for some reason, so that in spite of everything, it is still well to examine things a bit more closely.

There is no doubt that quietism in the proper sense of the word enjoys a bad reputation in the West, and first and foremost in the religious milieu; this is quite natural after all since the variety of mysticism so designated has been expressly declared heterodox, and justly so by reason of the numerous grave dangers it presents from various points of view, and which basically are only those of passivity itself raised to its highest pitch and put into practice 'integrally'— that is, without any attenuation of the consequences it entails in all orders. Thus there is no reason to be surprised if those for whom insults take the place of arguments, and who unfortunately are only too numerous, use quietism (as well as pantheism) as a sort of 'bogey', if we may so put it, to turn away those who might be influenced by what they themselves fear, a fear due merely to their inability to understand these things. But it is even more curious that the 'lay' mentality of the moderns readily turns this same accusation of quietism against religion itself, extending it improperly not only to all mystics—including the most orthodox among them—but also to monks of the contemplative orders, who moreover in their eyes are all classed together as 'mystics', although this may not necessarily be the case in reality; there are even some who push the confusion further still, going so far as to identify mysticism and religion, purely and simply.

This is easily explained by the prejudices generally endemic to the modern Western mentality; this latter, turned exclusively toward outward action, has come little by little not only to ignore on its own account all that relates to contemplation, but even to feel a true hatred toward it, wherever it is found. These prejudices are so widespread that many people who consider themselves religious, but who are still very much affected by this anti-traditional mentality, are apt to declare that they make a great distinction between the contemplative orders and those that occupy themselves with social action; for the latter they naturally have nothing but praise, but on the other hand are all too willing to agree with their adversaries in demanding that the former be suppressed on the pretext that they are no longer adapted to the conditions of an age of 'progress' like our own! And we should add in passing that even today such a distinction would be impossible in the Christian churches of the East, where no reason for wanting to become a monk can be conceived other than the desire to give oneself to contemplation, and where the contemplative life moreover, far from being foolishly accused of 'uselessness' and 'idleness', is on the contrary unanimously regarded as the superior form of activity that it truly is.

In this connection it must be said that in Western languages there is something rather awkward which, in a way, can contribute to certain confusions: this is the use of the words 'action' and 'activity', which, while obviously sharing a common root, have neither the same meaning nor the same scope. 'Action' is always meant as an outward activity that strictly speaking belongs to the corporeal order alone, and it is precisely this that distinguishes it from and in a way opposes it to contemplation, although here as elsewhere the point of view of opposition is necessarily illusory, as we have explained elsewhere, it being really a question of complementarity. 'Activity' on the other hand has a much more general meaning and applies equally in all domains and at all levels of existence: thus, to take the simplest example, one speaks of mental activity, but even with all the imprecision of current language one would hardly speak of mental action; and, in a higher order, one could just as well speak of spiritual activity, which is what contemplation is effectively (to be distinguished of course from simple meditation, which is only one means for achieving it and still pertains to the domain of the individual mentality). But there is more: if one considers the complementarity of 'active' and 'passive' in conjunction with 'act' and 'potency' taken in the Aristotelian sense, it is easy to see that what is most active is thereby also what is nearest the purely spiritual order, whereas it is passivity that predominates in the corporeal order. The consequence of this, which is paradoxical only in appearance, is that activity is all the greater and more real as it is exercised in a domain the more remote from that of action. Unfortunately, most moderns hardly seem to understand this point of view, and this results in such singular misunderstandings as that of certain orientalists who do not hesitate to qualify *Purusha* as 'passive', where the Hindu tradition is concerned, or *T'ien*, where the Far-Eastern tradition is concerned—that is, precisely what is on the contrary in each case the active principle of universal manifestation!

These few considerations allow one to understand how moderns are tempted to see 'quietism', or what they believe they can call by this name, in every doctrine that puts contemplation above action, that is, in the final analysis, every traditional doctrine without exception. Moreover, they seem to believe that in a way this is equivalent to despising action and even to denying it any proper value, even in its own contingent order, which is completely false since it is really only a matter of putting each thing in the place that normally belongs to it; to recognize that a thing occupies the lowest degree in a hierarchy does not in any way amount to denying its legitimacy, for it too is a necessary element in the whole of which it forms a part. We do not really know why it has become a habit to attack Hindu doctrine in particular on this point, since in this respect it does not differ in any way from other traditions, Eastern or Western; furthermore, on various occasions we have sufficiently explained how the Hindu tradition envisages action and need not dwell on it further here. Let us only point out how absurd it is to speak as some do of 'quietism' in reference to *yoga*, especially when one thinks of the prodigious activity that must be deployed in all domains to reach its goal (which in reality is *yoga* itself in its strict sense, the preparatory means being so designated only by extension); moreover this involves properly initiatic methods, of which activity is an essential characteristic. In order to forestall any possible objection let us add that if the interpretations of certain contemporary Hindus seem to lend themselves to the charge of 'quietism', this is because they are not in any way qualified to speak of these things, since, having received a Western education, they are almost as ignorant concerning their own tradition as are Westerners themselves.

But if the orientalists are in accord in reproaching Hinduism for despising action, they generally feel compelled to relate Taoism even more expressly to 'quietism'. This is because of the role played therein by 'non-action' (*wu-wei*), the real meaning of which they in no way understand, and which some of them make a synonym of 'inactivity', 'passivity', or even 'inertia' (it is because the active principle of manifestation is 'non-acting' that they maintain it is passive, as we said above). Nevertheless, there are those who have recognized that this is an error, but since they have no clearer understanding of what is involved and likewise confuse action and activity, they object to translating *wu-wei* as 'non-action' and replace the term by vague and insignificant circumlocutions that diminish the importance of the doctrine and leave nothing of its profounder and specifically initiatic meaning intact. In reality, the translation 'non-action' is the only acceptable one, but because of the usual incomprehension it is worthwhile to explain how this is to be understood. Not only is this 'non-action' not inactivity, but, following what we said above, it is on the contrary the supreme activity because it is as far removed as possible from the domain of outward action and is completely free of all the limitations imposed upon the latter by its own nature; if 'non-action' were not by very definition beyond all oppositions, it could be said that in a way it is the extreme opposite of the goal that quietism assigns to spiritual development.

It goes without saying that for the one who has reached it, 'non-action', or its equivalent in the initiatic part of other traditions, implies a perfect detachment with respect to outward action—as also with respect to all other contingent things, moreover—and this is because such a one lies at the very center of the 'cosmic wheel', whereas contingent things belong only to the circumference. If quietism for its part professes an indifference that in certain respects seems to resemble such detachment, this is assuredly for altogether different reasons. Just as similar phenomena can arise from very diverse causes, so ways of acting (or, in certain cases, abstaining from action) that are outwardly the same may proceed from the most varied motives, although for those who limit themselves to appearances, this can naturally give rise to many false assimilations. In this regard there are indeed certain facts, strange in the eyes of the profane, that can be invoked by them in support of the erroneous connection they wish to establish between quietism and traditions of an initiatic order; but this raises other questions interesting enough in themselves to merit dedicating the next chapter to them.

27

APPARENT MADNESS
AND HIDDEN WISDOM

AT THE END OF THE PRECEDING CHAPTER we alluded to certain rather extraordinary ways of acting that, depending on the case, can proceed from the most diverse causes. It is true that in general they always imply that the outer action in envisaged otherwise than it is by the majority of men, and that the action in and of itself is then not accorded the importance that would usually be attributed to it; but this requires a number of further distinctions. First of all, let us make clear that detachment regarding action (of which we spoke in connection with 'non-action') is above all a perfect indifference to the results one might obtain thereby, since, whatever these results may be, they can no longer really affect the being that has reached the center of the 'cosmic wheel'. Moreover, it is evident that such a being will never act out of a need to act, and if for any reason he must act—all the while fully conscious that his action has a merely contingent appearance, illusory as such from his own point of view, though not of course from that of its witnesses—he will necessarily not accomplish it in a way that differs outwardly from that of other men, unless there be particular motives for doing so in certain determinate cases. We can easily understand that this is entirely different from the attitude of Quietists and other 'irregular' mystics, who claim that action is unimportant (even though they are nowhere near the point where it appears as purely illusory) and therein discover a pretext for doing anything at all indiscriminately, following the impulses of the instinctive or 'subconscious' part of their being. Obviously, this risks leading to all kinds of abuses, disorders, and deviations, which at the very least pose the grave danger of allowing inferior possibilities to develop freely and without control, for the effort to overcome them is incompatible with the extreme passivity characteristic of this type of mystic.

One could also ask to what extent the indifference displayed in such cases is indeed genuine (and whether it can really be so for someone who has not reached the center, and been effectively freed by that fact from all 'peripheral' contingencies), for we sometimes see these same mystics given to perfectly deliberate extravagances: thus the Quietists properly speaking, namely those of the late seventeenth century, formed an association called 'Holy Childhood', in which they diligently imitated childish behavior and speech, their intention being to implement as literally as possible the Gospel precept of 'becoming like little children.' This is truly the 'letter that killeth', and it is surprising that a man like Fénelon was not reluctant to lend himself to such a parody—one is hardly able to describe it in any other way, as this imitation of children by adults is inevitably artificial and strained, and therefore something of a caricature. In any case, this simulation (for such it was) could hardly be reconciled with the quietest conception according to which it is necessary to keep consciousness separate from action, and therefore never prefer one mode of action to another. We do not mean to deny that a certain simulation, even of madness (which after all does not differ overmuch in appearance from the follies of childhood), may sometimes be justified, even in simple mystics; but this justification is possible only on the condition that one adopts a point of view completely different from that of quietism. We are thinking especially of certain cases frequently encountered in Eastern forms of Christianity where, it is worth noting, mysticism itself has not quite the same meaning as in the West. Indeed, 'Eastern hagiography' has some strange and unusual paths to sanctification, like that of the 'fools in Christ', whose extravagant acts are meant to hide their spiritual gifts from the eyes of onlookers under the shocking appearance of madness; or, rather, are meant to free them from the bonds of this world in their most intimate and most spiritually troublesome expression, that of the 'social ego'.[1] This appearance of

1. Vladimir Lossky, *The Mystical Theology of the Eastern Church* (Crestwood, NY: St. Vladimir's Seminary Press, 1976), p20.

madness can be an effective means, although not the only one, of escaping all indiscreet curiosity as well as any social obligations not really compatible with spiritual development; but it is important to note that this involves assuming an attitude toward the outer world that constitutes a kind of 'defense' against the latter, and not, as with the Quietists, a means that by itself leads to the acquisition of certain inner states. We must add that such a simulation is rather dangerous, for it can easily progress step by step toward genuine madness, especially in the mystic, who by definition is never entirely the master of his states; moreover, between mere simulation and actual madness there can be numerous degrees of rather marked disequilibrium, and any disequilibrium is necessarily an obstacle which, as long as it continues to exist, oppresses the harmonious and complete development of the higher possibilities of the being.

This leads us to consider another case, outwardly quite similar to the previous one even though it differs greatly from it in several fundamental respects: this is the case of the *majādhīb*, who indeed present themselves under an extravagant aspect very reminiscent of the just mentioned 'fools in Christ', but here it is no longer a case of simulation, or of mysticism, although it can very easily give the illusion of such to an outside observer. The *majdhūb* normally belongs to a *ṭarīqah*, and consequently has followed an initiatic path, at least through its early stages (and such a path, as we have often remarked, is incompatible with mysticism); at a certain moment however he is overwhelmed from the spiritual side by an 'attraction' (*jadhb*, whence the name *majdhūb*), which, for lack of adequate preparation and a sufficiently 'active' attitude, causes a disequilibrium, a sort of 'scission' as it were, among the different elements of his being. The higher part, instead of carrying the lower part with it, so that the latter might participate insofar as possible in its development, on the contrary detaches itself and leaves the latter behind,[2] so to speak, which can only result in a fragmentary and somewhat disjointed realization. Indeed, from the point of view of a complete

---

2. It is understood moreover that the link can never be entirely broken, for then death would immediately follow; but it is extremely weakened and 'slackened' as it were, which also happens to one degree or another in all cases of disequilibrium.

and normal realization, no element of the being is really unimportant, not even those which, belonging to a lower order, must thereby be considered to have a lesser reality (though not as having no reality at all); one need only know how to keep each thing in its proper place at all times within the hierarchy of the degrees of existence, something equally true of outward action, which is only the activity proper to certain of these elements. Through the failure to 'unify' his being, the *majdhūb* 'loses his footing' and becomes as if 'outside himself'; this is so because he is no longer the master of his states, which is the only respect in which he can be compared to the mystic; and though he may in reality be neither madman nor shammer (this latter term not necessarily having a pejorative sense here, as should already be evident from the preceding), he nonetheless often presents the appearance of madness.[3] In regard to the initiatic path, all of this is unquestionably a deviation, as is also the case, though of a somewhat different type, with those who produce more or less extraordinary 'phenomena', such as those one encounters notably in India; and, in addition to the fact that these cases have in common that spiritual development can never reach its perfection in them, we will presently discover still another reason for comparing them.

Our preceding remarks naturally apply to the true *majādhīb*, but there may also be false *majādhīb*, who intentionally take on the appearance of the former without really being so, which is why there is good reason to give the utmost attention to recognizing the essential distinctions involved, for this simulation can be of two entirely opposite kinds. On the one hand, there are the common shammers, whom one could also call 'counterfeiters', who profit in passing themselves off as *majādhīb* in order to lead a sort of 'parasitic' existence; these are obviously not of the slightest interest, being simple beggars who, like all false cripples and other simulators of this kind, show a certain special skill in the plying of their trade. On the other hand, it can also happen that a man who has attained a high degree of spiritual development conceals himself among the *majādhīb*; this he does for various reasons, but above all to pass unnoticed and

3. That is why, in ordinary language, the word *majdhūb* is sometimes used as a sort of 'euphemism' for *majnūn*, 'madman'.

unrecognized by the crowd for what he truly is; even a *walī* [a Sufi saint], in his relations with the outer world (relations whose nature and motives necessarily escape the appreciation of ordinary men), may sometimes also take on the appearance of a *majdhūb*. Nonetheless, except for their intention to remain hidden, such persons cannot be compared to the 'fools in Christ', who have not reached such a state and are only mystics of a particular type; and it goes without saying that the dangers we have stressed in this regard do not in the least exist here, since it is a case of beings whose real state can no longer be affected by these outward manifestations.

We must now point out that the same thing occurs with those producers of 'phenomena' to whom we alluded above, which leads directly to the case of 'jugglers', whose behavior has so often served in all traditional forms as a 'disguise' for initiates of high rank, especially when they had to fulfill some special worldly 'mission'. By 'juggler' we must not understand only a kind of 'conjurer', in accord with the very restricted meaning given this word by moderns, for from our vantage point the man who exhibits the most authentic psychic 'phenomena' belongs to exactly the same category, the juggler being one who amuses a crowd by accomplishing remarkable things, or even by simply affecting extravagant behavior.[4] This is how he was understood in the Middle Ages, when the juggler was thereby identified with the jester; moreover, we know that the jester was also called 'mad' (though he was not), which shows the rather close linkages among the various cases we have just described. If we should add that the juggler, as well as the *majdhūb*, is usually a 'wanderer', it becomes easy to understand the advantages offered by this role when for reasons of simple expediency, or for other much more profound reasons, one wishes to escape the attention of the profane or to divert it from that of which they should remain ignorant.[5] Indeed, madness—as the extreme opposite of wisdom—is

---

4. Etymologically, the juggler (from the Latin *joculator*) is literally a 'joker', whatever may be the type of 'jokes' he indulges in.

5. The juggler and the true *majdhūb* can also, by reason of the same advantages, serve to 'convey' certain things without being conscious of it themselves; but this is another question and does not concern us here.

one of the most impenetrable masks with which this latter can cover itself; that is why, in Taoism, when the 'Immortals' manifest themselves in our world, they are always described under a somewhat extravagant and even ridiculous aspect, not free even from a certain 'vulgarity'; but this last trait relates to yet another aspect of the matter.

28

THE 'POPULAR' MASK

As WE PREVIOUSLY noted, the 'Immortals' of Taoism are described under appearances that combine extravagance and vulgarity. The union of these two aspects can also be found elsewhere, notably in the *majdhūb* and the 'juggler', and consequently in those who borrow their outward appearance, all of whom while appearing to be 'mad' evidently also present a certain 'popular' character. These two aspects, however, are not necessarily linked, and it can also happen that the one called either 'vulgar' or 'popular' (these two words being basically synonymous) serves by itself as an initiatic 'mask'; that is, initiates, and especially those of the highest orders, can thereby easily hide themselves among the people, acting so as to avoid being outwardly noticeable. This is the most precise and complete application of the Rosicrucian precept that at all times one adopt the language and costume of the people among whom one is living, and wholly conform to their ways of acting, thereby making it possible to pass unnoticed among the profane, something not without importance in many respects, though there are other more profound reasons for such behavior.

This merits our close attention, for what is involved in such a case is always the people, and not what in the West is called the 'middle class' (or what more or less corresponds to it elsewhere); this is true to such a degree that in Islamic countries it is said that when a *Quṭb* is to manifest himself among ordinary men, he will often take on the appearance of a beggar or a peddler. Moreover, the same people—and this is certainly not an accidental conjunction—are entrusted with the preservation of truths of an esoteric order that would otherwise risk being lost; and since they are doubtless not capable of understanding them, such truths are thus transmitted all the more faithfully, even if in these circumstances they too must be concealed by a more or less crude mask (this being, in brief, the real origin and the true raison d'être of all 'folklore', especially of so-called popular tales). One may well ask how in this milieu—to which some do not hesitate to apply the pejorative 'lower classes'—the elite, and even the uppermost segment of the elite and thus in a sense the very opposite of the former, is able to find its best refuge, both for itself and for the truths of which it is the normal repository; but, although this seems paradoxical if not actually contradictory, we shall soon see that this is not at all the case in reality.

As long as the people have not suffered a 'deviation'—and as an eminently 'plastic' mass, corresponding to the 'substantial' side of what may be called the social entity, they could in no way be responsible for this—they bear within themselves, by virtue of this 'plasticity', the very possibilities that the 'middle class' lacks; and although these are assuredly only indistinct and latent possibilities— virtualities if you wish—they nonetheless exist, and given favorable conditions, are always capable of being developed. Contrary to current views, the people neither act spontaneously nor produce anything on their own; rather, they are like a 'reservoir' from which anything can be drawn, the best as well as the worst, according to the nature of the influences acting upon them. As to what can be expected from the 'middle class', this is all too easily determined if we reflect on the fact that it characterizes itself essentially by that narrowly limited 'common sense' that finds its most perfect expression in the concept of 'ordinary life', and that the most typical products of its mentality are the rationalism and materialism of the modern era, these latter giving the most exact measure of its possibilities, since such are the results when these possibilities are allowed to develop freely. We in no way deny that the middle class has been influenced by certain suggestions, for it too is 'passive', at least relatively speaking; but since it is no less true that this is where the above conceptions took form, thus where these suggestions met with fertile ground, this inevitably implies some correspondence to their own tendencies. And finally, if one is justified in calling it 'middle', is this not above all on condition that the word be invested with the sense of 'mediocrity'?

But there is yet something else, which completes our previous explanation and shows its full significance: the elite, by the very fact that the people is its extreme opposite, truly finds therein its most direct reflection (just as in all things the highest point is directly reflected not at any intermediate point but at the lowest point). Admittedly, it is an obscure and inverse reflection, as with the body with respect to the spirit, but it nonetheless offers the possibility of a 'rectification' comparable to that which takes place at the end of a cycle; for only when the descending movement has reached its limit, and thus its lowest point, can all things be immediately restored to the highest point in order to begin a new cycle. This is why it is correct to say that 'extremes meet', or, rather, that they rejoin. The analogy of the people to the body, to which we have just alluded, is further justified by the characteristics of the 'substantial' element that both present in the social and individual orders respectively, whereas the mental element, above all in its aspect of 'rationality', corresponds instead to the 'middle class'. Thus it follows that the elite, in descending as it were to the people, thereby discovers all the advantages of 'embodiment', insofar as this is necessary for the constitution of a truly complete being in our state of existence; and the multitude is for the elite a 'support' and a 'base', as is the body for the spirit in human individuality.[1]

The apparent identification of the elite with the multitude properly corresponds to what in Islamic esoterism is the principle of the *Malāmatiyah* [the Perfect Ones], who as a rule adopt an outward appearance that is all the more ordinary and common—and indeed even coarse—as their interior state is more perfect and their spiritually more elevated, and who, in their relations with other men, never allow anything of their spirituality to appear.[2] We can say that

1. Insofar as it involves a 'descent of the spirit', we can also compare this to the considerations we set forth at the end of chapter 31, 'The Two Nights'.

2. See Abdul-Ḥādi, 'Al Malāmatiyah', in the October 1933 issue of *Voile d'Isis*, and the appendix of the present work.

through this extreme contrast between the interior and the exterior they put the maximum 'interval' so to speak between these two aspects of their being, which allows them to comprehend within themselves the greatest number of possibilities of every order, which, at the terminus of their realization, logically results in the veritable 'totalization' of the being.[3] It must be understood that this contrast relates only to the world of appearances, for in absolute reality, and consequently also at the just mentioned terminus of realization, there is no longer any interior and exterior, for there too the extremes are finally rejoined in the Principle.

Moreover, it is particularly important to note that the 'popular' appearance adopted by initiates constitutes, at all degrees, a kind of image of 'descending realization';[4] this is why the state of the *Malā-matiyah* is said to 'resemble that of the Prophet, who was elevated to the highest degrees of the divine Proximity,' but who, 'when he returned to the people, spoke with them of external things only,' so that, 'from his intimate conversation with God, no trace appeared on his person.' If it is added that 'this state is superior to that of Moses, upon whose face no one could look after he had spoken with God,' this again refers to the idea of totality as explained above; it is basically an application of the axiom that 'the whole is more than any of its parts',[5] whatever the part may be, even if it be the most eminent of all.[6] In the case of Moses the 'redescent' is not in fact completely effected, if one may so put it, and does not fully integrate all the inferior levels, but extends only to the level symbolized by the outward appearance of common men, so that these latter

3. By this we do not mean to say that the totality can be realized in this way alone, but only that it can effectively be so in the mode proper to the way of the *Malāmatiyah*.

4. See the last chapter of the present work, 'Ascending and Descending Realization'.

5. We do not say 'greater', as one usually does—which restricts the axiom to its mathematical application only—for here one must obviously consider it as beyond the quantitative domain.

6. It is in like manner that we must understand the superiority of man's nature to that of the angels, such as it is envisaged in the Islamic tradition.

may participate in transcendent truth in the measure of their respective possibilities. In a way this is the inverse aspect of what we envisaged when we spoke of the people as a 'support' for the elite; it is also, of course, the complementary aspect, for to be effective this same role of 'support' necessarily requires a certain participation, so that each point of view implies the other reciprocally.[7]

Needless to say, the precept of avoiding any outward distinction from the multitude, while in reality differing from them most profoundly, is also found expressly in Taoism, and is formulated repeatedly by Lao Tzu himself;[8] here moreover it is very closely linked to a certain aspect of the symbolism of water, which always collects in the lowest places,[9] and, although nothing is weaker than it, yet it is able to overcome the strongest and most powerful of things.[10] Insofar as it is an image of the 'substantial' principle, water can, in the social order, also be a symbol of the people, and this corresponds well to its inferior position; thus the sage, in imitating the nature or character of water, becomes seemingly indistinguishable from the people; but this very fact, more than any other, allows him, not only to influence the entire multitude through his 'action of presence', but also to preserve intact and sheltered from all attack that by which he is inwardly superior to other men, and which moreover constitutes the only true superiority.

We have indicated only the main aspects of this very complex question, and will conclude with one last remark that relates more particularly to the Western esoteric traditions. It is said that those Templars who escaped the destruction of their Order concealed themselves among builders. Even though some are unwilling to see

---

7. The participation involved here is moreover not always limited exclusively to traditional exoterism; one can illustrate this by the example of those belonging to Islamic *ṭuruq*, who, in their most outward aspect (which, however, is still esoteric by definition) associate with elements that are properly 'popular' and which manifestly are not capable of anything more than a merely virtual initiation; and it seems this was also the case in the 'Thyiads' of Greek antiquity.

8. *Tao Te Ching*, especially chaps. 20, 41, and 67.

9. Ibid., chap. 8; cf. chaps. 41 and 46.

10. Ibid., chaps. 43 and 78.

in this anything but a 'legend', the event is no less significant for its symbolism; and it is undeniable that at least some Hermeticists, especially those connected with the Rosicrucian current, acted in this way.[11] In this connection we may further recall that among the initiatic organizations based on the practice of a craft, those that remained purely 'artisanal' underwent less of a degeneration than those affected by the intrusion of elements belonging mostly to the 'bourgeoisie'; and, apart from other reasons for this which we have given elsewhere, can we not see in this an example of that faculty of 'popular' conservation belonging to esoterism, of which 'folklore' is another manifestation?

11. It is clear that we make no allusion here to the supposed origins of the 'speculative' transformation of Masonry, which was really a degeneration, as we have sufficiently explained on other occasions, and that what we have in view goes back much earlier than the beginning of the eighteenth century.

29

THE MEETING
OF EXTREMES

WHAT WE JUST SAID about the relationship between the initiatic elite and the people still seems to call for further explanations of a complementary nature so as not to leave room for any ambiguity; and first of all it is necessary that no mistake be made as to the meaning of the word 'vulgarity' that we have employed in this connection. Indeed, if the word 'vulgar', taken in its original sense as in our discussion, is basically synonymous with 'popular', there is also an altogether different kind of vulgarity that corresponds more closely to the pejorative meaning usually attached to it in ordinary language, and the truth is that this latter meaning applies especially to the 'middle class'. To make what we are talking about immediately comprehensible, let us consider all the difference which A.K. Coomaraswamy[1] has so well noted between 'popular' art and 'bourgeois' art,[2] or again, regarding things intended for everyday use, between the products of artisans of former times and those of modern industry.

---

1. Modern industry is indeed very much the work of the 'middle class', which created it and directs it, and it is for this very reason that its products can satisfy only those needs from which all spirituality is excluded, in conformity with the notion of 'ordinary life'; this seems to us too evident to require further emphasis.

2. See especially 'Primitive Mentality' [reprinted in *Coomaraswamy, Vol. 1: Selected Papers, Traditional Art and Symbolism*, ed. Roger Lipsey (Princeton: Princeton University Press, 1977)]. Let us also recall moreover the use Dante made of the word 'vulgar' in his treatise *De Vulgari Eloquentia*, and especially his expression *vulgare illustre* (see 'Nouveaux aperçus sur la langage secret de Dante' in the July 1932 issue of *Voile d'Isis* [*Insights into Christian Esoterism*, chap. 6]).

This remark leads us back to the *Malāmatiyah*, whose name derives from the word *malāmah*, meaning 'blame';[3] but what must we understand by this? From the traditional point of view their actions are not actually blameworthy in themselves, which is all the more inconceivable given that, far from neglecting the prescriptions of the *sharī'ah*, they on the contrary apply themselves especially to teaching those around them by example as well as by words. However, because their way of acting is not in any way distinguishable from that of the people,[4] it appears blameworthy in the eyes of a certain 'opinion', which is above all precisely that of the 'middle class', or of persons who consider themselves 'cultured', according to the expression so much in vogue today. The concept of profane 'culture', on which we have often made our position clear,[5] is indeed very characteristic of the mentality of this 'middle class', to which, by its wholly superficial and illusory 'brilliance', it gives the means of concealing its true intellectual nullity, and this same class is also that which enjoys invoking 'custom' in every circumstance. It goes without saying that the *Malāmatiyah*, or those in other traditions who behave similarly, are hardly disposed to take into account this 'custom', which lacks any significance or spiritual value, nor consequently to worry themselves over an 'opinion' that esteems only empty appearance.[6] It is certainly not here that the 'spirit', or the elite who represent it, can find a point of support, for all these things reflect absolutely nothing spiritual, being much rather the negation of all spirituality. On the contrary, where the reflection of the spirit is found—even if it be inverted, as every reflection necessarily must be—there also is its normal 'support', whether it be the body in the individual order, or the people in the social order.

As we have pointed out, it is precisely because the highest point is reflected in the lowest that it can be said that extremes meet; in this

3. They are also called *ahlul-malāmah*, literally 'people of blame', that is, those who expose themselves to blame.

4. Exoteric law itself can be called 'vulgar' if one takes this word in the sense of 'common', in that it applies to all without distinction; besides, are there not in our day, and nearly everywhere, all too many who think they prove their 'distinction' by abstaining from the accomplishment of traditional rites?

5. See *Perspectives on Initiation*, chap. 33.

6. See chapter 4, 'Custom Versus Tradition'.

connection we have recalled the comparison that can be made with what occurs at the end of a cycle, and this too is a matter requiring more explanation. Indeed, it must be carefully noted that the 'rectification' by which the return from the lowest to the highest point is accomplished is properly speaking 'instantaneous', which is to say that in reality it is intemporal, or, better still—so as not to restrict ourselves to the consideration of the particular conditions of our world—outside of all duration, which implies a passage through the non-manifested; this constitutes the 'interval' (*sandhyā*), which, according to the Hindu tradition, always exists between two cycles or two states of manifestation. If it were otherwise, the beginning and the end could not coincide in the Principle, when it is a question of the totality of manifestation, or could not correspond to one another, when only particular cycles are under consideration. Moreover, by reason of its 'instantaneity', there is really no interruption in this passage, which is just what allows one to speak of a true meeting of extremes, although the meeting point necessarily escapes all more or less exterior means of investigation because it lies outside the series of successive modifications that constitute manifestation.[7]

For this reason it is said that any change of state can only be accomplished in darkness,[8] the color black in its superior sense being the symbol of the non-manifested; but in its inferior sense this same color also symbolizes the indistinction of pure potentiality or the *materia prima*;[9] and here again these two aspects, although they must in no way be confused, nevertheless correspond analogically and are associated in a certain way, according to one's point of view. All 'transformation' appears as a 'destruction' when considered from the point of view of manifestation; and what is in reality a return to the principial state seems to be, if seen from without and from the 'substantial' side, a 'return to chaos', just as from the same point of view the origin, although proceeding directly from the Principle, takes on the appearance of 'emerging from

7. We intend to return to this point in connection with the symbolism of the 'chain of the worlds'.

8. See *Perspectives on Initiation*, chap. 26.

9. See below, 'The Two Nights'.

chaos'.[10] Moreover, since every reflection is necessarily an image of what is reflected, the inferior aspect may be considered as representing the superior aspect in its own relative order, on condition of course that we not forget the principle of 'inversion'; and this, which is true of the relationships between spirit and body, is no less true of those between the elite and the people.

The existence of the people, or of those confused with it in appearance, is, in current language itself, an 'obscure' existence; and even though those who use it are doubtless unaware of this, the term in fact expresses the 'substantial' character inherent to the role that belongs to it in the social order; from this point of view it has, we will not say the total indistinction of *materia prima*, but at least the relative indistinction of what fulfills the function of *materia* at a certain level. It is an entirely different matter for the initiate who lives among the people without being outwardly distinct from them. Like one who hides his wisdom under the no less 'obscure' appearance of madness, he can, in addition to the various advantages he may find therein, see in this very obscurity an image as it were of the 'higher darkness'.[11] One can draw from this yet another consequence: if initiates occupying the highest ranks of the spiritual hierarchy take no visible part in the events that unfold in this world, this is above all because such 'peripheral' action would be incompatible with their 'central' position; if they hold themselves entirely aloof from every 'mundane' distinction, this is obviously because they know the emptiness of such things; but it can also be said that if they were to consent thus to emerge from their obscurity, their exterior would by this very fact no longer really correspond to their interior, so that if this were possible the result would be a sort of

10. In alchemical symbolism, every 'transmutation' presupposes the passage through a state of indifferentiation that is represented by the color black, and that may equally well be considered under these two aspects.

11. This can also be compared to what we have said elsewhere concerning the higher meaning of anonymity (cf. *The Reign of Quantity and the Signs of the Times*, chap. 9), the latter being equally 'obscure' for the individual; but at the same time it represents liberation from the individual condition and is even a necessary consequence of it, since name and form (*nāma-rūpa*) are strictly constitutive of individuality as such.

disharmony in their very being. However, since the spiritual degree they have attained necessarily excludes such a supposition, it also excludes the possibility of their effectively consenting to this.[12] Moreover, it goes without saying that what is involved here has nothing in common with 'humility', and that the beings of whom we speak are well beyond the sentimental domain to which the latter essentially belongs; but here again is a case where things outwardly similar may in reality proceed from entirely different causes.[13]

To return to the point that particularly concerns us at present, we will say this: the 'black blacker than black' (*nigrum nigro nigrius*), according to the Hermeticists' expression, is assuredly, when taken in its most immediate and most literal sense, indeed the obscurity of chaos or of the 'lower darkness'; but it is also, and by this very fact, a natural symbol of the 'higher darkness', as we have just explained.[14] Just as 'non-action' is really the fullness of activity, or as 'silence' contains within itself all sounds in their *pārā*, or non-manifested, modality, this 'higher darkness' is in reality the Light that surpasses all light, that is, beyond all manifestation and every contingency, the principal aspect of light itself; and it is here, and here only, that the true meeting of extremes is finally accomplished.

---

12. It is worth recalling in this connection what we have said elsewhere on the 'rejection of powers' (*Perspectives on Initiation*, chap. 22); in fact, these 'powers', although of a different order, are nonetheless contrary to the 'obscurity' of which we have just spoken.

13. There is no question of denying that humility can be considered a virtue from the exoteric, and especially the religious, point of view (which of course includes that of the mystics); but from the initiatic point of view, neither humility nor the pride that is its correlative can any longer have meaning for one who has surpassed the domain of oppositions.

14. Expressions like 'black heads' or 'black faces', met with in various traditions, also present a double sense, comparable to this in certain respects. Perhaps we will one day have occasion to return to this question. [See *Symbols of Sacred Science*, chap. 16, 'The Black Heads'. ED.]

30

IS THE SPIRIT
IN THE BODY
OR THE BODY
IN THE SPIRIT?

THE ORDINARY CONCEPTION according to which the spirit is considered to be housed within the body cannot fail to seem very strange to anyone who possesses even the most elementary metaphysical knowledge, not only because the spirit cannot truly be 'localized', but because, even if this is only a more or less symbolic 'manner of speaking', it seems at first glance to imply a manifest illogicality and a reversal of normal relationships. Indeed, the spirit is no other than *Ātmā*, which is the principle of all states of the being, at all degrees of its manifestation. Now all things are necessarily contained in their principle, and they can in no way depart from it or enclose it within their own limits; it is therefore all the states of the being, and consequently also the body—which is merely a modality of one of these states—that must finally be contained in the spirit, and not the reverse. The 'lesser' cannot contain the 'greater', any more than it can produce it; and this principle is applicable at different levels, moreover, as we shall see later; but for the moment we are considering the most extreme case, that which concerns the relationship between the very principle of the being and the most restricted modality of its individual human manifestation. One might be tempted to conclude immediately that the current conception arises only from the ignorance of the great majority of men and merely corresponds to a simple error of language, which everyone repeats by force of habit and without reflection; but the question is in fact not so simple, and this error, if it is one, has other causes which are much more profound than one might at first believe.

Of course, it must first of all be understood that the spatial image of 'container' and 'content' must never be taken literally, since only one of the two terms under consideration, the body, really possesses a spatial character, space itself being neither more nor less than one of the conditions proper to corporeal existence. The use of such spatial, as well as temporal, symbolism is nonetheless, as we have many times explained, not only legitimate but even inevitable, since we must use a language that belongs to corporeal man and is therefore itself subject to the conditions determining the existence of the latter as such; it suffices to never forget that anything not belonging to the corporeal world could by this very fact be neither in space nor in time.

On the other hand, it is of little importance to us that philosophers should have felt obliged to discuss such a question as that of the 'seat of the soul', apparently taking this in a completely literal sense; moreover, given the habitual confusion of modern Western language in this respect, what they call 'soul' could really be the spirit, at least to the degree that they conceive of this. It goes without saying that for us profane philosophers are certainly in no way distinct from the common run of people, and that their theories have no more value than mere public opinion; and so it is assuredly not their so-called 'problems' that could lead us to think that some sort of 'localization' of the spirit in the body could be anything other than a pure and simple error; but the traditional doctrines themselves show the insufficiency of leaving it at that, and the need for examining this subject more deeply.

Indeed, according to Hindu doctrine we know that *jīvātmā*, which is really *Ātmā* itself considered more particularly in relation to the human individuality, resides at the center of this individuality, and is designated symbolically as the heart. This is not of course to say that it is enclosed in the corporeal organ bearing this name, or even in the corresponding subtle organ, but it no less truly implies that it is in some way situated within the individuality, and even more precisely within its centermost part. *Ātmā* can in truth be neither manifested nor individualized, nor, with all the more reason, can it be embodied; as *jīvātmā,* however, it appears to be individualized and embodied, an appearance that can obviously be only illusory with respect to *Ātmā* but nonetheless does exist from a certain point of view—the very point of view from which *jīvātmā* seems distinct from *Ātmā,* which is that of individual human manifestation. From this point of view, then, it can be said that the spirit is situated in the individual; and from the more particular point of view of the corporeal modality of the latter it can also be said that it is even situated in the body, on condition that this not be taken as a literal 'localization'. This manner of speaking is therefore not strictly an error but only the expression of an illusion that, although being such with respect to absolute reality, still corresponds to a certain degree of reality, that of the states of manifestation to which it relates; it only becomes an error when one tries to apply it to the total being, as if the principle of the latter could itself be affected or modified by one of its contingent states.

We have just made a distinction between the integral individuality and its corporeal modality, the former including all the subtle modalities as well; and in this regard we might add an observation that, although only accessory, will no doubt help with an understanding of what we chiefly have in view. For the ordinary man, whose consciousness is as it were 'awake' only in the corporeal modality, what is more or less dimly perceived of the subtle modalities appears to be contained within the body, this perception corresponding effectively only to their connections with the body and not to what they are in themselves. In reality, however, they cannot be thus contained in the body, and as it were confined by its limits, first of all because they are the immediate principle of the corporeal modality, and then again because they are susceptible of an incomparably greater extension by the very nature of the possibilities they comprise. Thus, when these modalities are effectively developed, they appear as 'prolongations' extending in all directions beyond the corporeal modality, which is thus as if entirely enveloped by them; for the one who has realized his integral individuality there is then a kind of 'reversal' in this regard, as compared with the point of view of the ordinary man. In the case we are considering, individual limitations have moreover not yet been surpassed, which is why we spoke earlier of a possible application at different levels; by analogy it can now be understood that a 'reversal' also occurs in another order when the being passes to supra-individual realization. As long as the being has only attained *Ātmā* in its connection with the individuality, that is, as *jīvātmā*, *Ātmā* appears to be enclosed in this individuality, and cannot even appear otherwise to the individuality since the latter is incapable of passing beyond the limits of the individual condition; but when *Ātmā* is attained directly and as it is in itself, this same individuality, along with all the other states, individual or supra-individual, now appear on the contrary as contained in *Ātmā*—as in fact they are from the point of view of absolute reality, since they are nothing other than the very possibilities of *Ātmā*, outside of which nothing can truly be in any mode whatsoever.

In the preceding we explained the limits within which, from a relative point of view, it is true to say that the spirit is contained in the human individuality, or even in the body; and we also indicated the reason why this is so, a reason that in the final analysis inheres in the very condition of the being for which this point of view is legitimate and valid. But this is still not all, and it must be pointed out that the spirit is envisaged as located not only in the individuality generally, but at its central point, to which the heart corresponds in the corporeal order. This requires further explanations, which will allow us to link together the apparently opposing points of view that relate respectively to the relative and contingent reality of the individual, and the absolute reality of *Ātmā*. It is easy to understand that these considerations must rest essentially on the application of analogical inversion, an application that at the same time illustrates in a particularly clear way the precautions required in transposing spatial symbolism, since, contrary to what holds in the corporeal order, that is to say in space understood in its strict and literal sense, in the spiritual order it is the interior that envelops the exterior, and the center that contains all things.

One of the best 'illustrations' of analogical inversion is provided by the representation of the different heavens corresponding to the superior states of the being, by as many circles or concentric spheres, as is found in Dante for example. In this representation it seems at first that if the heavens are greater—that is, less limited— to the extent that they are higher, they are also more 'exterior' in the sense that they are further from the center, the latter being constituted by the terrestrial world. This is the point of view of human individuality, represented precisely by the earth, and this point of view is true in a relative way insofar as this individuality is real in its own order and constitutes the starting-point from which the being must begin its ascent to higher states. But when the individuality is transcended, the 'reversal' we spoke of (and which is really a 'rectification' of the being) takes place, and the entire symbolic representation is as it were turned inside out: then the highest of all heavens is at the same time the most central since the universal center itself resides in it, and on the contrary it is now the terrestrial world that is located at the outermost periphery. In addition, it must be noted that in this 'reversal' of situation the circle corresponding to the highest heaven must nonetheless remain the greatest and must envelop all the others (as, according to Islamic tradition, the divine 'Throne' envelops all the worlds); it must be so, since in absolute reality it is the center that contains all. The impossibility of materially representing this point of view, where the greatest is at the same time the centermost, only illustrates the inevitable limitations to which geometrical symbolism is subject due to the fact that it is only a language borrowed from the spatial condition, that is, from one of the conditions proper to our corporeal world, and consequently linked exclusively to the other point of view, that of human individuality.

As concerns the center, it is clear from the inverse relationship between the true center (which is either that of the total being or of the Universe, depending on whether it is regarded from the 'microcosmic' or 'macrocosmic' point of view) and the center of the individuality or of its particular domain of existence how, as we have explained on other occasions, what is first and greatest in the principial order becomes in a certain way (without however being in any way altered or modified in itself) the last and the least in the order of appearances.[1] Continuing our use of spatial symbolism, this is finally the relationship of the geometrical point to what might be

---

1. Cf. the texts of the Upanishads which we have cited in different places on this matter, as well as the Gospel parable of the 'grain of mustard seed'.

called analogically the metaphysical point. This latter is the true primordial center, which contains within itself all possibilities, and is therefore what is greatest; having no 'location', because nothing can contain or limit it, all things are on the contrary located with respect to it (and it goes without saying that this again must be understood symbolically, since it is not a question of spatial possibilities alone). As for the geometrical point, which is located in space, it is evidently even in the literal sense the smallest of things since it is without dimension, that is, strictly speaking occupies no extension at all; but this spatial 'naught' corresponds directly to the metaphysical 'all', and it could be said that these are the two extreme aspects of indivisibility, envisaged respectively in the principle and in manifestation. As concerns the 'first' and the 'last', it suffices to recall here what we explained earlier, that the highest point has its direct reflection in the lowest; and to this spatial symbolism can be added a temporal symbolism, according to which the first in the principial domain, and consequently in 'no-time', appears as the last in the development of manifestation.[2]

It is easy to apply all this to what we considered at the outset: it is indeed the spirit (*Ātmā*) that is truly the universal center containing all things;[3] but when reflected in human manifestation it thereby appears as 'localized' at the center of the individuality, and even, more precisely, at the center of its corporeal modality, for this latter is the terminus of human manifestation and is therefore also its 'central' modality, so that with respect to the individuality this center is indeed the direct reflection and representation of the universal

2. In the Islamic tradition the Prophet is at once 'the first of God's creation' (*awwal khalqi 'Llah*) as to his principial reality (*an-Nūr al-Muḥammadī*), and the 'seal [that is, the last] of the messengers of God' (*Khātam rusuli 'Llah*) as to his terrestrial manifestation; he is thus also the 'first and the last' (*al-Awwal wa 'l-Ākher*) with respect to creation (*bin-nisbati lil-Khalq*), just as Allah is 'the First and the Last' in the absolute sense (*mutlaqan*). — In the Christian tradition, likewise, the Word is the 'Alpha and Omega, the beginning and the end' of all things. [See *Perspectives on Initiation*, chap. 47. ED.]

3. In this connection let us recall that in the Islamic tradition the primordial Light (*an-Nūr al-muḥammadī*, as mentioned in the previous note) is also the Spirit (*ar-Rūḥ*), in the total and universal meaning of this word; furthermore, one knows that the Christian tradition identifies the Light with the Word itself.

center. This reflection is assuredly only an appearance, as is individual manifestation itself; but as long as a being is limited by individual conditions, this appearance is reality for it, and it cannot be otherwise since this reality is of exactly the same order as its present consciousness. It is only when a being has gone beyond these limits that the other point of view becomes real for it, just as it is (and always has been) absolutely; its center is thenceforth in the universal, and the individuality (and even more so the body) is only one of the possibilities contained in this center; and by the 'reversal' so effected, the true relationships among things are re-established, such as they never ceased to be for the principial being.

We will add that this 'reversal' is closely connected with what kabbalistic symbolism calls the 'displacement of lights', and also with the saying that Islamic tradition puts in the mouth of the *awliyā*: 'Our bodies are our spirits and our spirits are our bodies' (*ajsāmnā arwāhnā, wa arwāhnā ajsmānā*), which indicates not only that all the elements of the being are wholly unified in the 'Supreme Identity', but also that the 'hidden' has become the 'visible', and inversely. Also, according to Islamic tradition, the being that has passed to the other side of the *barzakh* is in some way the opposite of ordinary beings (and this again is a strict application of inversion analogous to that of Universal Man and individual man): 'If he walks on sand he leaves no trace; if he walks on rock his feet leave their imprint.[4] If he stands in the sun he projects no shadow; in darkness a light emanates from him.'[5]

---

4. This has an evident connection with the symbolism of 'footprints' on rock, which goes back to 'pre-historic' epochs, and which is found in almost every tradition; without entering here into overly complex considerations, we can say that, in a general way, these footprints represent the 'trace' of the higher states in our world.

5. Let us also recall that the spirit corresponds to light and the body to darkness or night; it is then the spirit itself that envelops all things within its own radiance.

31

THE TWO NIGHTS

We do not intend to speak here of what the mystics call the 'night of the senses' and the 'night of the spirit'; although these may present partial similarities with what we shall discuss, they contain many elements difficult to 'situate' exactly, and they often even contain elements of a rather 'troubling' character, which obviously arises from the imperfections and limitations inherent to every merely mystical realization and which we have explained enough on other occasions not to have to address anew here. On the other hand, neither is it our intention to consider the three symbolic 'nights' representing three deaths and rebirths that, as concerns the human being, refer respectively to the corporeal, psychic, and spiritual orders.[1] The reason for this symbolism, which naturally is applicable to successive degrees of initiation, is that every change of state is produced through a phase of obscuration and 'envelopment', from which it results that this 'night' can be considered in as many hierarchical meanings as the very states of the being; but for the present we shall confine ourselves to only the two extreme senses. Indeed, what we propose to do is to explain more clearly how the symbolism of 'darkness' in its most general traditional usage presents two opposite meanings, one higher and one lower, and, in addition, to explain the nature of the analogical relationship existing between the two meanings which allows their apparent opposition to be resolved.

In its higher meaning, darkness represents the non-manifested, as we have already explained in the course of our present studies.

---

1. Cf. A. K. Coomaraswamy, 'Notes on the Kaṭha Upaniṣad', pt. 1 [*New Indian Antiquary*, April, May, and June 1938].

This presents no difficulty, but it seems nonetheless that the higher meaning is generally unknown or misunderstood, for it is easy to show that when it is a question of darkness, only its lower meaning is commonly considered; and often a 'malefic' significance is added that is by no means essentially inherent to it and is justified only for certain secondary and much more particularized aspects. In reality, the lower meaning represents 'chaos', the state of indifferentiation or indistinction that is the starting-point of manifestation, whether in its totality or relative to one of its states; and here we immediately see the application of analogical inversion, for this indifferentiation, which in Western language can be called 'material', is like the reflection of the principial indifferentiation of the non-manifested, what is at the highest point being reflected at the lowest point like the summits of the two opposed triangles in the symbol of the 'seal of Solomon'. We shall have to return to this later; but what must particularly be understood before going further is that when this indistinction relates to the totality of universal manifestation, it is nothing other than the indistinction of *Prakriti* insofar as this latter is identified with primordial *hyle* or with the *materia prima* of the ancient Western cosmological doctrines; in other words, it is the state of pure potentiality, which is nothing but a kind of reflected and thereby inverted image of the principial state of non-manifested possibilities; and this distinction is particularly important, for the confusion between possibility and potentiality is the source of innumerable errors. On the other hand, when it is only a question of the original state of a world or of a state of existence, potential indistinction can only be considered in a relative and already 'specified' sense in virtue of a kind of similarity between the process of development of universal manifestation and that of each of its constituent parts, a similarity which is expressed notably in cyclic laws. This can be applied at all degrees, and to the case of a particular being as well as to that of a more or less extensive domain of existence, and it corresponds to the remark we made above about a multiplicity of hierarchical meanings, for it goes without saying that because of their very multiplicity these meanings can only be relative.

From what has just been said it follows that the lower meaning of darkness is of a cosmological order while its higher meaning is of a properly metaphysical order; it can also be noted at this point that their relationship allows us to understand the fact that the origin and development of manifestation can be envisaged at one and the same time in an ascending and a descending sense. If this is so, it is because manifestation does not proceed only from *Prakriti*, from which its entire development is a gradual passage from potency to act and can be described as an ascending process; in reality it proceeds from the two complementary poles of Being, that is from *Purusha* and *Prakriti*, and with regard to *Purusha* its development is a gradual separation from the Principle, thus a true descent. This consideration implicitly contains the solution to many apparent antinomies, especially those concerning cosmic cycles the course of which, one could say, is regulated by a combination of tendencies that correspond to these two opposed—or rather complementary— 'movements'. The developments this might occasion obviously lie outside our subject; but from the foregoing it can at least be easily understood that there is no contradiction at all between assimilating the starting-point or original state of manifestation to darkness in its lower sense, on the one hand, and on the other, the traditional teaching about the spirituality of the 'primordial state', for the two do not relate to the same point of view but respectively to the two complementary viewpoints we have just described.

We have considered the lower meaning of darkness as the reflection of its higher meaning which indeed it is from a certain point of view; but at the same time, from another point of view it is also as it were its 'reverse', taking this word in the sense in which the 'reverse' and 'obverse' are opposed to each other like the two faces of one same thing; and this requires further explanation. The point of view relating to the reflection is naturally that of manifestation and every being situated in the domain of manifestation; but from the standpoint of the Principle, where the origin and end of all things meet and unite, there can no longer be a question of reflection since here there is really only one single thing, for the starting-point of manifestation as well as its endpoint are necessarily in the non-manifested. From the point of view of the Principle in itself, if one can still use such a manner of speaking, one cannot even distinguish two aspects of a single reality since such a distinction only arises and is valid for manifestation; but if the Principle is considered in its relationship to manifestation one can distinguish two faces as it were, which correspond to the going out from and the return to the non-manifested. Since return to the non-manifested is the final end of manifestation, it can be said that, when viewed from this point, the non-manifested appears as darkness in the higher sense, while when viewed from the starting-point of manifestation it appears on the contrary as darkness in the lower sense; and depending on the way in which the 'movement' of manifestation with respect to non-manifestation is effected it can also be said that the higher face is turned toward the Principle while the lower face is turned toward manifestation, although this image of two faces seems to imply a kind of symmetry which cannot truly exist between Principle and manifestation, and further, there can obviously be in the Principle itself no distinction between higher and lower. The point of view of the reflection is illusory with regard to the Principle, just as the reflection itself is illusory with regard to what is reflected; thus this point of view of the two faces corresponds to a deeper reality although it is itself illusory at another level since it in turn disappears when the Principle is considered in itself and no longer in relation to manifestation.

The point of view we have just described might become clearer if one considers what corresponds to it within manifestation in the passage from one state to another. This passage is in itself a single point, but it can naturally be envisaged from both of the two states between which it is situated and of which it is the common limit. Here again one thus finds the two faces: this passage is a death with regard to one of these states while being a birth with regard to the other; but this death and birth coincide in reality and the distinction between them exists only in regard to the two states, one of which has its end and the other its beginning in this same point. There is an evident analogy with what, in the preceding considerations, concerned not two particular states of manifestation but total manifestation itself and the Principle, or more precisely the passage from one to the other; moreover it is appropriate to add here that one also finds analogical inversion, for on the one hand birth into manifestation is like a death to the Principle, whereas on the other, inversely, death to manifestation is a birth, or rather, is a 're-birth', into the Principle, so that beginning and end are inverted according to whether they are considered in relation to the Principle or in relation to manifestation. This of course is always said concerning the relation of one to the other, for in the immutability of the Principle itself there is certainly neither birth nor death nor beginning nor end, but it itself is the first beginning and the last end of all things without there being any distinction at all between this beginning and this end in absolute reality.

If we now consider the case of the human being we can ask what, for him, corresponds to the two 'nights' between which all of universal manifestation unfolds. As for the higher darkness, there is once again no difficulty here, for whether it be a matter of a particular being or of the totality of beings it can never represent anything else than the return to the non-manifested; because of its strictly metaphysical character this meaning remains unchanged in all the applications which can be made of this symbolism. But as concerns the lower darkness, it is obvious that here it can only be taken in a relative sense, for the starting-point of human manifestation does not coincide with that of universal manifestation but rather occupies a determinate level within it. What appears as 'chaos' or as potentiality can thus be so only relatively and in fact already possesses a certain degree of differentiation and of 'qualification'; it is no longer *materia prima* but, if one likes, a *materia secunda* that plays an analogous role for the level of existence under consideration. Moreover, it goes without saying that these remarks do not apply only to a being but also to a world; it would be an error to think that potentiality pure and simple could be found at the origin of our world, which is but one degree of existence among others; despite its state of indifferentiation, the *ākāsha* nonetheless is not devoid of all quality, and it is already 'specified' in view of the production of corporeal manifestation alone; it can therefore never be confused with *Prakriti,* which, being absolutely undifferentiated, thereby contains in itself the potentiality of all manifestation.

From this it follows that, as to what represents the lower darkness in the human being, only the image of reflection—to the exclusion of that of the two faces—can be applied in relation to the higher darkness. Indeed, every level of existence can be taken as a plane of reflection, and it is only because the Principle is in some way reflected there that it possesses any reality at all, that of which it is capable in its own order; but on the other hand, if one passes to the other face of the lower darkness one will not be in the Principle or in the non-manifested, but only in a 'pre-human' state which is nothing but another state of manifestation. Thus we are brought back to what we explained earlier about the passage from one state to another: on the one hand it is birth into the human state and on the other it is death to the 'pre-human' state; or, in other words, it is the point which, depending on the side from which it is considered, appears as the final point of one state and the starting-point of the other. Now, if the lower darkness is taken in this sense, it could be asked why, in a symmetrical way, the higher darkness is not simply considered to represent death to the human state, or the end of this state, which does not necessarily coincide with a return to non-manifestation but can be merely a passage to another state of manifestation, for the symbolism of night indeed applies, as we have said, to every change of state whatsoever. But, besides the fact that this would be only a very relative 'superiority', since the beginning and end of a state are only two points situated at consecutive levels separated by an infinitesimal distance along the 'axis' of the being, this is not what matters from the point of view we have chosen. What must be essentially considered is the human being as he is presently constituted in all his integrality, with all the possibilities he carries within himself; but among these possibilities is that of directly attaining the non-manifested, which indeed he already touches, if one can so speak, in his higher part, and this part, not itself human properly speaking, is nonetheless that which makes him exist as human since it is the very center of his individuality; and in the condition of the ordinary man this contact with the non-manifested appears in the state of deep sleep. Moreover, it must be clearly understood that this is in no way a 'privilege' of the human state, and that if one considered any other state one would always find there this same possibility of a direct return to the non-manifested without passing through other states of manifestation, for existence in any state is only possible due to the fact that *Ātmā* resides at the center of this state, without which it would vanish like pure nothingness. This is why, at least in principle, every state can be equally taken as the starting-point or as a 'support' of spiritual realization, for in the universal or metaphysical order all contain in themselves the same virtualities.

Once one adopts the viewpoint of the constitution of the human being, the lower darkness then appears more under the aspect of a modality of that being rather than under the aspect of a first 'moment' of its existence; but in a certain sense the two things meet, for what is involved here is the starting-point of the development of the individual, a development that has different phases corresponding to his different modalities which thereby possess a certain hierarchy; it is thus what can be called a relative potentiality, starting from which the integral development of the individual manifestation is effected. In this respect, what is represented by the lower darkness can only be the grossest part of the human individuality, the most 'tamasic' in a way, but that in which this individuality in its entirety is nonetheless enveloped as in a seed or embryo; in other words, this will be nothing other than the corporeal modality itself. Moreover, it should not be surprising that, in the human being, it is the body that corresponds to the reflection of the non-manifested, for here again a consideration of analogical inversion allows all apparent difficulties to be immediately resolved. The highest point, as we have already said, is necessarily reflected at the lowest; and this is why, for example, in our world principial immutability finds its inverted image in the immobility of minerals. In general it can be said that the properties of the spiritual order are expressed in what is most corporeal, but 'turned inside out' and 'negatively' as it were; fundamentally this is only an application to this world of what we explained earlier about the inverse relationship of the state of potentiality to the principial state of non-manifestation. By virtue of the same analogy the state of wakefulness, in which the consciousness of the individual is 'centered' in the corporeal modality, is spiritually a state of sleep, and inversely; this consideration of sleep, moreover, enables one to better understand that the corporeal and the spiritual appear to one another as 'night', although naturally it is illusory to consider them symmetrically as two poles of the being even if only because the body is not really a *materia prima* at all but a mere 'substitute' for it relative to a determinate state, while the spirit never ceases to be a universal principle and never is situated at any relative level. If these reservations are taken into account and if one is speaking in conformity to the appearances inherent in a certain level of existence, one can speak of a 'sleep of the spirit' corresponding to the corporeal wakefulness; the 'impenetrability' of bodies, as strange as this may seem, is itself only an expression of this 'sleep', and moreover all their characteristic properties could equally be interpreted from this analogical point of view.

With regard to realization, what must above all be kept in mind from these considerations is that, if it is achieved from the human state, it is the body itself that must serve as its basis and starting-point; this is its normal 'support', contrary to certain prejudices current in the West which would see in it only an obstacle or treat it as a 'negligible quantity'. The application of this to the role of corporeal elements in all rites, as means or aids toward realization, is too obvious to need emphasis here. Furthermore, there would certainly be many other consequences to draw from all of this which we cannot develop at present; in particular one can glimpse the possibility of certain transpositions and 'transmutations' quite unexpected by those who have never dreamed of such possibilities; but of course it is not according to the modern 'mechanistic' and 'psycho-chemical' theories of the body that any of this could ever be understood.[2]

---

2. In Islamic tradition the two 'nights' we have spoken of are represented respectively by *laylatul-qadr* and *laylatul-mirāj*, corresponding to a double 'descending' and 'ascending' movement: the second is the nocturnal ascension of the Prophet, that is to say a return to the Principle through the different 'heavens' which are the superior states of the being. As for the first, it is the night in which the descent of the Koran occurred, and that 'night', according to the commentary of Muḥyi 'd-Dīn ibn al-'Arabī is identified with the very body of the Prophet. What is especially to be noted here is that the 'revelation' is received, not in the mind but in the body of the being that has a 'mission' to express the Principle: *Et Verbum caro factum est* [And the Word was made flesh], says the Gospel also (*caro* and not *mens*), and this, very exactly, is another expression, in a form proper to Christian tradition, of what *laylatul-qadr* represents in Islamic tradition.

32

ASCENDING
AND DESCENDING
REALIZATION

IN THE TOTAL REALIZATION of the being, there is good reason to look at the union of the two aspects which, in a way, correspond to two phases of this realization, one 'ascending' and the other 'descending'. Consideration of the first phase in which a being, starting from a certain state of manifestation, ascends to identification with its unmanifested principle, cannot raise any difficulty, since it is universally and expressly indicated as the process and essential goal of all initiation, this latter ending at the 'emergence from the cosmos', as we have explained in previous articles, and, consequently, to liberation from the limiting conditions of every particular state of existence. On the contrary, concerning the second phase of 'redescent' into the manifested, it seems that it is rarely spoken of, and in most cases in a less explicit way, sometimes even with a certain hesitancy and reserve which the explanations given below will allow one to understand. Doubtless this is why misunderstandings easily arise, so that one either wrongly regards this way of envisaging things as more or less exceptional, or is mistaken as to the real character of the 'redescent' involved.

First of all we will consider what could be called the question of principle, that is, the very reason why every traditional doctrine, provided that it is presented in a truly complete form, cannot, in reality, view things otherwise, and this can be understood without difficulty if one refers back to the teaching of the *Vedānta* on the four states of *Ātmā*, as they are specifically described particularly in the *Māndūkya Upanishad.*[1] Indeed, it is not only the three states represented in the human being by wakefulness, dream, and deep sleep, that correspond respectively to corporeal manifestation, subtle manifestation, and the unmanifested itself; but beyond the three states, therefore beyond the unmanifested, is a fourth, which may be called 'neither manifested nor unmanifested', since it is the principle of both, but which also, because of that, includes both the manifested and the unmanifested. Now, although the being really attains his own 'Self' in the third state, that of the unmanifested, the ultimate end is not this state, but the fourth, in which alone the 'Supreme Identity' is fully realized, for *Brahma* is at once both 'being and non-being' (*sadasat*), 'manifested and non-manifested' (*vyaktāvyaktaḥ*), 'sound and silence' (*shabdāshabda*), without which It would not truly be absolute Totality; and if realization were to stop at the third state, it would involve only the second of the two aspects, that which language can express only in a negative form. Thus, as A. K. Coomaraswamy said in a recent study:

> While one must have gone beyond the Manifested (Sun) [which is represented by the passage 'beyond the Sun'] to reach the unmanifested (Darkness [understood in its higher sense]), the Person and last end lies beyond the Unmanifested; one has not reached the end of the road until one knows Him [*Ātmā*] as Manifested and Unmanifested (*vyaktāvyaktaḥ*),[2]

so that to reach this end, it is necessary to pass 'beyond the darkness', or, as expressed in certain texts, 'to see the other aspect of darkness'. Otherwise, *Ātmā* can 'shine' in itself, but does not 'radiate'; it is identical to *Brahma*, but in a single nature, not in the double nature which is included in His unique essence.[3]

Here it is necessary to anticipate a possible objection: it could be pointed out that there is no common measure between the manifested and the unmanifested, so that the first is as nothing beside the second, and, moreover, that the unmanifested, already being in itself

1. See *Man and His Becoming according to the Vedānta*, chaps. 12 through 17.
2. 'Notes on the Kaṭha Upaniṣad', pt. 3. [*New Indian Antiquary*, June 1938, p210.]
3. Cf. *Brihandāranyaka Upanishad*, II.3.

the principle of the manifested, must consequently contain it in some way. All of this is perfectly true, but it is no less true that the manifested and the unmanifested, so long as they are envisaged thus, still appear in a way as two terms between which there exists an opposition, and this opposition, even if it is only illusory (as moreover all opposition basically is) must nonetheless ultimately be resolved; now it cannot be so except by passing beyond one or other of its two limits. Furthermore, if the manifested cannot be called real in the absolute sense of the word, it nevertheless possesses within itself a certain reality, relative and contingent no doubt, but a reality to some degree, since it is not pure nothingness, which would after all be inconceivable, for that would exclude it from universal Possibility. Therefore one cannot finally say that the manifested is strictly negligible, although it may seem so with respect to the unmanifested, and that this may even be one of the reasons why what relates to it in realization can sometimes be less conspicuous, as if expelled to the darkness. Finally, if the manifested is in principle included in the unmanifested, it is as the totality of the possibilities of manifestation, but not as the effectively manifested. In order that manifestation also be included in this last respect, we must, as we said, return to the principle common to the manifested and the unmanifested, which is truly the supreme Principle from which everything proceeds and within which everything is reconciled; and as will be more plainly seen in what follows, this has to be so for there to be full and total realization of the 'Universal Man'.

Another question now arises: from what we have just said, it is a case of different stages in the course of one and the same way, or more accurately, of one stage and of the final end of that way, and it is quite evident that it must indeed be so, since it is the realization which is thereby carried on to its ultimate conclusion. But in all this how can we speak, as we did at first, of an 'ascending' phase and a 'descending' phase? It goes without saying that if both representations are legitimate they must relate to different points of view in order not to be contradictory. However, before seeing how they can effectively be reconciled, we can already note that in any case, reconciliation is possible only on condition that the 'redescent' is not in any way conceived as a sort of 'regression' or 'turning back', which would moreover also be incompatible with the fact that everything acquired by the being in the course of initiatic realization is so in a permanent and definitive way. Thus, there is nothing here comparable to what happens in the case of transitory 'mystical states' such as 'ecstasy', after which the being again finds itself purely and simply in terrestrial human existence, with all the individual limitations that condition it, and in its present consciousness, retaining only an indirect and always more or less imperfect reflection of these states.[4] It is hardly necessary to say that the 'redescent' in question is not comparable to what is designated as the 'descent into Hell'. The latter, as is known, takes place prior to the beginning of the actual initiatic process, and in exhausting certain inferior possibilities of the being, it plays a 'purifying' role which would manifestly no longer have any raison d'être later on, especially on the level referred to in the present discussion. So as not to pass over in silence any possible misunderstanding, let us further add that there is absolutely nothing in common there with what could be called a 'backwards realization', which would have meaning only if it took this 'descending' direction starting from the human state, but the direction of which would then be properly 'infernal' or 'satanic', and consequently could only arise from the domain of the 'counter-initiation'.[5]

That said, it becomes easy to understand that the point of view from which the realization in its entirety appears as the traversing of a way that is so to speak 'rectilinear' is that of the very being that is accomplishing it, since for that being there could never be any question of going backwards and returning to the conditions of one of

---

4. We should add in this connection that something similar may also take place in a case other than that of 'mystical states', which case is a true metaphysical realization, but remaining incomplete and still virtual. The life of Plotinus offers an example of this which is no doubt the best known. In the language of the Islamic *taṣawwuf*, it is thus a case of a *ḥāl* or transitory state which has not been able to be fixed and transformed into a *maqām*, that is, into a permanent 'station' acquired once and for all, whatever be the degree of realization to which it corresponds.

5. The course of such a 'descending' way, with all the consequences it implies, cannot even be envisaged effectively to the whole extent possible, except in the extreme case of the *awliyā ash-Shaytān* [saints of Satan] (Cf. *The Symbolism of the Cross*, p 114, n 1).

the states it has already surpassed. As for the point of view from which this same realization takes on the aspect of the 'ascending' and 'descending' phases, it is merely that from which the realization can appear to other beings who view it while themselves remaining in the conditions of the manifested world. However, it may still be asked how a continuous movement can thus take on, even outwardly, the appearance of a unity of two movements succeeding one another in opposite directions. Now there exists a geometric representation which allows one to get as clear an idea of this as possible: if we consider a circle placed vertically, the course of one of the halves of the circumference will be 'ascending', and that of the other half 'descending', without the movement ever ceasing to be continuous. Moreover, in the course of that movement there is no 'turning back', since it does not again pass through the part of the circumference which it has already traversed. Here we have a complete cycle, but if we remember that truly closed cycles cannot exist, as we have explained on other occasions, we realize by that very fact that it is only in appearance that the end-point coincides with the starting-point or, in other words, that the being returns to the manifested state from which it had started (an appearance which exists for others, but which is in no way the 'reality' of this being). Moreover, this consideration of the cycle is all the more natural here in that what is involved has its exact 'macrocosmic' correspondence in the two phases of 'inhalation' and 'exhalation' of universal manifestation. Finally, it can be noted that a straight line is the 'limit', in the mathematical sense of the word, of a circumference which increases indefinitely. The distance traversed in the realization (or rather what is represented by a distance when spatial symbolism is used) being truly beyond all assignable measure, there is in reality no difference in the length of the circumference of which we spoke previously and that of an axis which remains vertical in all its successive parts; and this completes the reconciliation of the representations corresponding respectively to the 'interior' and 'exterior' points of view which have been differentiated.

By these diverse considerations, it may now be thought possible to understand sufficiently the true character of the apparently descending phase; but regarding the initiatic hierarchy, the question still remains as to what the difference can be between the realization arrested at the 'ascending' phase and that which in addition includes the 'descending' phase; it is this above all which will have to be examined in what follows.

While the being remaining in the unmanifested has accomplished realization solely 'for itself', the one that later 'redescends' in the sense previously made clear, has from then on, with respect to manifestation, a role that expresses the symbolism of the solar 'radiation' by which all things are illuminated. In the first case, as we have already said, *Ātmā* 'shines' without 'radiating'. However, here it is necessary to dispel yet another misunderstanding. In this regard we speak too frequently of an 'egoistical' realization, which is veritable nonsense, since there is no longer any *ego*, that is, individuality, the limitations constituting the latter having necessarily been abolished in definitive fashion, in order that the being may be able to 'establish itself' in the unmanifested. Such a misunderstanding evidently implies a gross confusion between the Self and the 'ego'. We said that this being has achieved realization 'for itself', and not 'for himself', and this is not a simple question of language, but a distinction that is altogether essential as to the very root of what is in question. That said, there nonetheless remains a difference between the two cases, the true importance of which can be better understood by referring to the way in which various traditions envisage the states that correspond to each, for even if the 'descending' realization as a phase of the initiatic process is generally indicated only in a more or less veiled way, one can nevertheless easily find examples where it is clearly taken for granted without any possible doubt.

First of all, to take perhaps the best known if not generally the best understood example, the difference in question is finally that which exists between the *Pratyēka-Buddha* and the *Bodhisattva*.[6] In this regard, it is particularly important to note that the way which has the first of these two states as its end is designated as a 'small way' or, if one wishes, a 'lesser way' (*hinayāna*), thus implying that it is not exempt from a certain restrictive character, whereas the one

---

6. The case of the *Pratyēka-Buddha* is one of those to which Western interpreters readily apply the term 'egoism', the absurdity of which we have just indicated.

leading to the second state is considered to be truly the 'greater way' (*mahāyāna*), and therefore the one that is complete and perfect in all respects. This allows us to answer the objection which could arise from the fact that in a general way the state of *Buddha* is regarded as superior to that of *Bodhisattva*. In the case of the *Pratyēka-Buddha*, that superiority can only be apparent, and it is due above all to the character of 'impassiveness' which, apparently, the *Bodhisattva* does not have; we say 'apparently' because it is necessary to differentiate between the 'reality' of the being and the role it has to play with respect to the manifested world, or in other words, between what it is in itself and what it appears to be for ordinary beings. Moreover, we will find the same distinction to be made in cases belonging to other traditions. It is true that, exoterically, the *Bodhisattva* is represented as having yet one last stage to cross in order to attain the state of a perfect *Buddha*, but if we say exoterically, it is precisely because it corresponds to the way things appear when they are viewed from the outside. It is necessary that it should be so in order that the *Bodhisattva* may fulfill his function insofar as this is to show the way to other beings: he is 'the one who went this way' (*tathā-gata*), and this is the way they must go who, like him, are able to attain the supreme goal. Thus it is necessary that in order to be truly 'exemplary', the very existence in which he accomplishes his 'mission' should be presented in some manner as a recapitulation of the way. As for claiming that it is really a case of a still imperfect state or of a lesser degree of realization, this is to lose sight entirely of the 'transcendent' aspect of the being of the *Bodhisattva*. This is perhaps in conformity with certain current 'rational' interpretations, but it renders perfectly incomprehensible all the symbolism concerning the life of the *Bodhisattva* which confers upon him from his very beginning a properly 'avataric' character, that is, shows it effectively as a 'descent' (this is the correct meaning of the word *avatāra*) by which a principle, or a being representing the latter because identified with it, is manifested in the exterior world, which obviously is in no way able to alter the immutability of the principle as such.[7]

---

7. One could say further that such a being, laden with all the spiritual influences inherent to its transcendent state, becomes the 'vehicle' by which those same

What we have said above has to a very large extent its equivalent in the Islamic tradition, taking into account the difference in the points of view which are naturally proper to each of the diverse traditional forms; and this equivalent is found in the distinction made between the case of the *walī* [saint] and that of the *nabī* [prophet]. A being can be a *walī* only 'for himself', if one is thus permitted to express oneself, without manifesting anything of it on the exterior, while a *nabī*, on the contrary, is only such because he has a function to fulfill with regard to other beings; and this is true for all the more reason of the *rasūl*, who is also a *nabī*, but whose function bears a character of universality, while that of the simple *nabī* can be more or less limited in respect of its extent and proper goal.[8] It could even seem that the apparent ambiguity that we saw just now regarding the *Bodhisattva* should not exist here since the superiority of the *nabī* with respect to the *walī* is generally admitted and even regarded as evident; and yet, it has sometimes been maintained that the 'station' (*maqām*) of the *walī* is, in itself, higher than that of the *nabī*, because it essentially implies a state of 'divine proximity', whereas the *nabī*, by his very function, is necessarily turned toward creation. Here again, this is to see only one of the two faces of the reality, the exterior, and not to understand that it represents one aspect which is added to the other without in any way destroying or

---

influences are directed toward our world. That 'descent' of spiritual influences is quite explicitly indicated by the name *Avalokiteshvara*, and it is also one of the principal and 'benefic' meanings of the inverted triangle. Let us add that it is precisely with this meaning that the inverted triangle is taken as the symbol of the highest grades of Scottish Masonry. In the latter, the 30th degree, being regarded as *nec plus ultra* [nothing beyond that], must thereby logically mark the limit of the 'ascent', so that the following degrees can only properly refer to a 'redescent', by which the influences destined to 'invigorate' it are brought to the whole initiatic organization. The corresponding colors, which are respectively black and white, are again very significant in this respect.

8. The *rasūl* manifests the divine attribute of *ar-Raḥmān* [the Compassionate] in all the worlds (*raḥmatan lil-ʿālamīn*), not just in a certain particular domain. — It can be noted that the designation of *Bodhisattva* as 'Lord of Compassion' also relates to a similar role, as 'compassion' extended to all beings is fundamentally only another expression of the attribute of *raḥmah*.

even really affecting it.[9] Indeed, the condition of the *nabī* implies first of all in itself that of the *walī*, but it is at the same time something more; thus in the case of the *walī* there is a sort of 'lack' in a certain respect, not as to his intimate nature, but as to what could be called his degree of universalization, a 'lack' which corresponds to what we said concerning the being that stops at the stage of the unmanifested without 'redescending' toward manifestation. The universality attains its effective plenitude in the *rasūl*, who is thus truly and totally 'Universal Man'.

In cases such as those just cited, one can see clearly that with regard to manifestation the being that 'redescends' has a function of which the somewhat exceptional character clearly shows that it does not find itself back in a condition comparable to that of ordinary beings. Thus these cases are those of beings whom one could describe as charged with a 'mission' in the true sense of the word. In a certain sense, one can also say that every manifested being has its 'mission', if by this one simply understands that it must occupy its proper place in the world and that it is thus a necessary element of the totality of which it is a part; but it goes without saying that it is not understood in this way here, but rather as a 'mission' of an altogether different scope, proceeding directly from a principial and transcendent order and expressing something of that same order in the manifested world. As the 'redescent' presupposes the previous ascent, such a 'mission' necessarily presupposes perfect inner realization. It is useful to emphasize this, especially at a time when many people too easily imagine themselves to have more or less extraordinary 'missions', which, lacking this essential condition, can only be pure illusions.

Even after all the considerations put forward so far, we must still discuss one aspect of the 'redescent' which in many cases seems to

9. The following refers to what was said on the notion of *barzakh* [isthmus], which allows one to understand without difficulty how these two faces of reality are to be understood. The inner face is turned toward *al-Ḥaqq* [The Truth], and the outer face toward *al-khalq* [creation]. The one whose function is of the nature of the *barzakh* must necessarily unite in himself these two aspects, thus establishing a 'bridge' or a 'canal' by which divine influences spread to the creation.

explain the fact that this subject is passed over in silence or surrounded by reticence, as if there were something there of which one were loathe to speak clearly: what is involved is what could be called its 'sacrificial' aspect. It must be clearly understood that here the word 'sacrifice' is not used in the simply 'moral' sense commonly given to it, and which is only one of the examples of the degeneration of modern language, diminishing and misrepresenting all things in order to reduce them to a purely human level and make them fit within the conventional frameworks of 'ordinary life'. On the contrary, we take this word in its true and original sense, with all that it includes that is effectively and even essentially 'technical'. Indeed, it goes without saying that the role of beings such as those in the case previously cited could not have anything in common with 'altruism', 'humanitarianism', 'philanthropy', and other 'ideal' platitudes extolled by moralists, which are not only too evidently lacking in any transcendent or supra-human character, but are even perfectly within reach of any profane person who comes along.[10]

The being having realized its identity with *Ātmā* and its 'redescent' into manifestation (or what appears as such from the point of view of the latter, but which is effectively only the full universalization of that very identity), is then none other than '*Ātmā* incorporated into the worlds'. This amounts to saying that for it the 'redescent' is in reality nothing different from the very process of universal manifestation. Now, this process is often traditionally described as a 'sacrifice'; in the Vedic symbol, it is the sacrifice of *Mahāpurusha*, that is of 'Universal Man', with whom, according to what we have already said, the being in question is effectively identical. Not only must this primordial sacrifice be understood in the

10. It must be made clear that what we are saying here concerns the specifically modern point of view of 'lay morality'. Even when, as often happens in spite of its pretensions, the latter in some way only 'plagiarizes' precepts borrowed from religion, it empties them of all real meaning, brushing aside all the elements which would allow them to be linked to a higher order and, beyond the simply literal exoterism, be transposed as signs of principial truths. Sometimes even, while seeming to retain what could be called the 'materiality' of those precepts, this morality actually goes so far as to 'turn' them in an anti-traditional direction by the interpretation it gives them.

strictly ritual sense, and not in a more or less vaguely 'metaphorical' sense, but it is essentially the very prototype of every sacrificial rite.[11]

The one charged with a 'mission', in the sense we gave this word previously, is thus literally a 'victim'; moreover, it is clearly understood that generally speaking this in no way implies that his life must end by a violent death, since in reality it is that same life in its entirety which is already the consequence of sacrifice.[12] It can immediately be noted that here we have the profound explanation of the hesitations and 'temptations' which in all traditional accounts, whatever the more particular form they assume according to the case, are attributed to Prophets, and even to *Avatāras*, when they are in some way brought face to face with the 'mission' they have to accomplish. Fundamentally, these hesitations are none other than those of *Agni* to accept becoming the driver of the 'cosmic chariot',[13] as Coomaraswamy says in the study already cited, thus linking all these cases to that of the 'eternal *Avatāra*' with whom they are but one in their most inner 'truth'; and assuredly, the temptation to remain in the 'night' of the unmanifested can be

11. In this regard a remark can be made in passing which is not without importance: the life of certain beings, considered according to individual appearances, presents facts which are in correspondence with those of the cosmic order and which from the exterior point of view are as it were an image or a reproduction of the latter. From the interior point of view, this relationship must be inverted, for since these beings are really *Mahāpurusha*, it is cosmic facts that are truly modelled on their life, or, to speak more exactly, on that of which their life is a direct expression, while the cosmic facts in themselves are only a reflected expression of it. We will add that this is also what bases in reality and renders valid the rites instituted by those invested with a 'mission', whereas a being that is nothing more than a human individual will never, on its own initiative, be able to make up anything but 'pseudo-rites' lacking any real effectiveness.

12. It should also be noted that what is involved is unrelated to the use that certain mystics readily make of the words 'victim' or 'sacrifice', even in cases where what is meant thereby has a proper reality and is not reduced to simple 'subjective' illusions—always possible with them by reason of the 'passivity' inherent in their attitude. It is a reality of which the range in no way goes beyond the order of individual possibilities.

13. *Rig-Vēda*, x.51.

understood without any difficulty, for none would contest that in this superior sense, 'night is better than day'.[14] With good reason, Coomaraswamy thereby also explains the fact that Shankarāchārya always visibly strives to avoid consideration of the 'redescent', even when commenting on texts where it is clearly implied. Indeed, in a case like this it would be absurd to attribute such an attitude to a lack of knowledge or to an incomprehension of the doctrine; and therefore it can only be understood as a sort of recoiling before the perspective of 'sacrifice', and consequently, as a conscious desire not to lift the veil which conceals 'the other face of darkness'; and to generalize from what we were just saying, this is the principal reason for the customary discretion on this question.[15] Moreover, one can add as a secondary reason the danger that this poorly-understood idea might serve as a pretext for some people who, by deluding themselves as to its true nature, justify a desire to 'remain in the world'; but in reality it is not a matter of remaining there, but, what is completely different, of returning to it after having already left it, and this previous 'going out' is possible only for the being in whom there no longer subsists any desire, nor any other individual attachment whatsoever. One must be very careful not to be mistaken on this essential point, for otherwise there is the risk of seeing no difference between ultimate realization and a simple beginning of realization arrested at a stage that has not even surpassed the limits of individuality.

Now, to return to the idea of sacrifice, we must add that it includes yet another aspect, the very one directly expressed by the

---

14. This expression also has its application in another order, in the 'rejection of powers', but whereas this attitude is not only justified but is even the only entirely legitimate one for a being which, not having any 'mission' to fulfill, does not have to appear outwardly, it is obvious that on the contrary, a 'mission' would be non-existent as such if it were not manifested outwardly.

15. As an 'illustration' of this, we will recall a fact the historical or legendary character of which matters little from our point of view, for we intend to give it only an exclusively symbolic value: it is said that Dante never smiled, and that people attributed this apparent sadness to the fact that he 'returned from Hell'. Should one not rather have seen that the true reason was that he had 'redescended from Heaven'?

etymology of the word, which is properly *sacrum facere*, that is, 'to render sacred' the object of the sacrifice. This aspect is no less appropriate here than is the one considered more ordinarily, which is the aspect we had in view at the beginning when we spoke of the 'victim' as such. Indeed, it is the sacrifice that confers a 'sacred' character, in the most complete sense of the term, upon those invested with a 'mission'. Not only is this character evidently inherent to the function of which their sacrifice is truly the investiture; but more— for this is also implied in the original sense of the word 'sacred'—it is what makes of them beings 'set apart', that is, essentially different both from the generality of manifested beings and from those which, having attained realization of the 'Self', remain purely and simply in the unmanifested. Their action, even when outwardly similar to that of ordinary beings, in reality has no connection with them going beyond simple outward appearance; in its 'truth' it is necessarily incomprehensible to individual faculties, for it proceeds directly from the inexpressible. This character again clearly shows that, as has already been said, it is a question of exceptional cases, and in fact those in the human state invested with a 'mission' are assuredly only a tiny minority with respect to the immense multitude of beings who could not lay claim to such a role. On the other hand, since the states of being are of an indefinite multiplicity, what reason can there be which would prevent admitting that, in one state or another, every being has the possibility of reaching this supreme degree of the spiritual hierarchy?

APPENDICES

CHAPTER 5

THE passage from *Pages dédiées à Mercure* of Abdul-Ḥādi reads as follows:

> *The two initiatic chains:* One is historical, the other spontaneous. The first is spread in known and established Sanctuaries under the direction of a living authorized *Shaykh* (*Guru*), who possesses the keys to the mystery. Such is the *At-Talīmur-rajāl* or instruction of men. The other is *at-Talīmur-rabbāni* or dominical or lordly instruction, which I venture to call 'Marian initiation' since it is that received by the Holy Virgin, mother of Jesus, son of Mary. There is always a master, but he can be absent, unknown, even dead for several centuries. In this initiation you draw from the present the same spiritual substance that others draw from antiquity. It is presently rather frequent in Europe, at least in its lower degrees, but it is almost unknown in the East.

This text was published in the review *La Gnose*, num. 10, of January, 1911. When we decided to reprint it in *Études Traditionelles* we asked René Guénon if he would be willing to write a note in order to prevent possible errors of interpretation. He sent us the following note, to which he alludes in chapter 5, note 11 of the present work.

As this paragraph might occasion certain misunderstandings, it seemed to us necessary to clarify its meaning a bit. First of all, it must be understood that what is involved here is nothing that could be assimilated to a 'mystical' way, which would obviously be contradictory to the affirmation of the existence of a real 'initiatic chain' in this case as well as in that which can be considered 'normal'. In this connection we may cite a passage of Jalāl al-Dīn Rumi which relates to exactly the same thing: 'If anyone by a rare exception has traversed this [initiatic] way alone [that is to say without a *Pīr*, a Persian term equivalent to the Arab *Shaykh*], he has arrived by the help of the hearts of the *Pīrs*. The hand of the *Pīr* is not refused to one who is absent; this hand is nothing other than the embrace of God.' (*Mathnavī* 1, 2974–5). In these last words can be seen an allusion to the role of the true interior *Guru* in a sense perfectly in conformity with the teaching of the Hindu tradition; but this takes us rather far from the question that directly occupies us here. We will say that from the point of view of Islamic *taṣawwuf*, what is involved is the way of the *Afrād*, whose Master is *Seyyidna Al Khidr*,[1] and is outside of what one might call the jurisdiction of the 'Pole' (*al-Quṭb*) which includes only the regular and usual paths of initiation. It cannot be too much emphasized that these are only very exceptional cases, as is expressly declared in the text just cited, and that they occur only in circumstances which make normal transmission impossible, for example in the absence of any regularly constituted initiatic organization. On this subject, see also the closing pages of *East and West*.

On the same subject we extract a few lines from a letter René Guénon addressed to us on March 14, 1937:

Al-Khidr is properly the Master of the *Afrād*, who are independent of the *Quṭb* and may not even be known by him; it is indeed as you say a matter of something more 'direct' and in a way outside defined and delimited functions no matter how elevated they may be; and this is why the number of the *Afrād* is indeterminate. This comparison is sometimes used: a prince, even if he exercises no function, is nonetheless higher in himself than a

---

1. *Al-Khidr* is the designation given by Islamic esoterism to the anonymous person mentioned in the Koran, surat 18 (surat of the Cave) with whom Moses, who is nonetheless considered by Islam as the law-bearing messenger and 'Pole' of his age, appeared in a relationship of subordination. This subordination appears to be both with regard to hierarchy and with regard to Knowledge, since the mysterious person is presented as possessing the most transcendent science (literally 'the science of Our Abode' [*chez Nous*], that is, of Allah) and since Moses only asks this person to teach him a part of the teaching in his possession. [Note by Jean Reyor.]

minister (at least if the minister is not himself a prince, something that can happen but which is not at all necessary); in the spiritual order the *Afrād* are analogous to princes and the *Aqtāb* to ministers. This is only a comparison, of course, but all the same it helps somewhat in understanding the relation of the ones to the others.

CHAPTER 28

We know give extracts from the study by Abdul-Ḥādi entitled *al-Malāmiyah* to which René Guénon returns in note 2 on page 143.

On this subject, here is an extract from the *Treatise on the Categories of Initiation* by Muḥyi 'd-Dīn ibn al-'Arabī:

'The fifth degree is occupied by "those who bow", those who humble themselves before the Lordly Grandeur, who take on themselves the priestliness of worship, who are exempt from every claim to any recompense in this world or in the other. These are the *Malāmiyah*. They are the "trusted men of God" and they constitute the highest group. Their number is not limited but they are placed under the direction of the *Quṭb* or "spiritual Apogee".[2] Their rule obliges them not to display their merits or to hide their defects. . . . They say that Sufism is humility, poverty, the 'Great Peace', and contrition. They say that "the face of the Sufi is downcast [literally 'black'] in this world and in the other," thus indicating that ostentation falls with pretension and that sincerity of adoration is manifested by contrition, for it is said, "I am near those whose hearts are broken because of Me." What they possess by grace comes from the very source of divine favors. Thus they no longer have either name or personal traits, but they are effaced in the *true prostration*.'

---

2. Nor is the number of the *Afrād* or 'solitaries' limited, but they are not under the surveillance of the *Quṭb* of the age. They form the third category in the esoteric hierarchy of Islam.

Abdul-Ḥādi next cites fragments of the treatise entitled *Principles of the Malamatiyah by the learned Imam, the wise Initiate, Sayed Abu Abdur-Rahman (grandson of Ismail ibn Najib)*:

As they have realized (the 'Divine Truth') in the higher degrees (of the Microcosm), as they have been affirmed among 'the men of concentration',[3] of the *Al-Qurbah*, the *Al-Uns*, and the *Al-Wasl*,[4] God is (so to speak) too jealous of them to let them reveal themselves to the world as they really are. So he gives them an appearance that corresponds to the state of 'separation from Heaven',[5] an appearance made of ordinary knowledge, of Shariite preoccupations—ritual or priestly—as well as the obligation to work, to follow a profession, and to act among men. Nevertheless, their interiors remain in continual connection with the 'True-Divine', as much in concentration (*al-jarq*) as in dispersion (*al jam'*), that is to say in all the states of existence. This mentality is one of the highest man can attain even though nothing of it appears on the outside. It resembles the state of the Prophet—may Allah pray for him and proclaim him!—who was raised to the highest degrees of the 'Divine Proximity' indicated by the Koranic formula, 'And he was distant by two lengths of a bow or even closer.'[6] When they turn toward creatures they speak with them only of outward things. Of their intimate conversation with God, nothing appears on their person. This state is higher than that of Moses, whose face no one could look upon after he had spoken with God. . . . The *Shaykh* of the group of Abu-Hafs en-Nisabūrī said: 'The Malamite disciples progress by exerting themselves. They care not for themselves. The world has no hold on them and cannot reach them, for their outer life is all uncovered while the subtleties of their inner life are rigorously hidden. . . .' Abu-Hafs was one day asked 'why the name Malamatiyah?' He

3. Ahlul-Jam'i.
4. Spiritual Union.
5. *Al-iftirāq.*
6. See Koran 53:9. The two bows are *al-'Ilm* and *al-Wujūd*, that is Knowledge and Being. See F. Warrain on Wronski, *La Synthèse concrète*, p169.

responded: 'The Malamatiyah are continually with God by the fact that they always dominate themselves and never cease to be conscious of *their lordly secret*. They blame themselves for all that they cannot prevent from showing with regard to their "Divine Proximity", in the office of prayer or otherwise. They conceal their merits and expose what is blameworthy in themselves. People then make their outward appearance a point of accusation; they blame themselves inwardly for they understand human nature. But God favors them by uncovering the mysteries, by the contemplation of the hypersensible world, by the art of knowing the intimate reality of things from outward signs (*al-ferāsah*), as well as by miracles. The world finally leaves them in peace with God, removed from them by their display of what is blamable or contrary to respectability. Such is the discipline of the *ṭarīqah* of the people of blame.'[7]

7. These words of Abu-Hafs were collected by Abdul-Hassan al-Warrāq who reported them to Ahmad ibn Aïssa, who in his turn was the source of information for Abu Abdur-Raḥmān, the author of the present treatise.

INDEX

Made in the USA
Lexington, KY
27 July 2013